PRAISE FOR *VLOG LIKE A BOSS*

"Mastering the art of the 'jab' through vlogging means learning from Amy Schmittauer. I don't consume a lot of video, but Amy knows how to crush it to get attention. She got mine. Take notes."

—Gary Vaynerchuk, Four-Time *New York Times* Best-Selling Author and CEO of Vaynermedia

"If you want to say, "Wow, I love my boss," then Amy Schmittauer is your girl! I'm so happy to call her an internet friend, and now you can too! Amy is charming, witty, smart, and fun as she drops all the vlog knowledge you need in one place. She's the best #VlogBoss ever!"

—Justine "iJustine" Ezarik, YouTuber and *NYT* Best-Selling Author

"Amy Schmittauer is the most authoritative voice in the how-to vlogging space. She is by far one of my favorite thought leaders and educational resources for all things digital and video. Her mentorship has contributed to my growth and success as a social media marketer and video producer."

—Tyler Culbertson, Social Media Manager for Tony Robbins

"The art of vlogging looks deceptively simple, but Amy does a masterful job of navigating through the many, many subtleties that turn a decent vlog into a great one."

—Austin Evans, YouTuber

"With *Vlog Like a Boss*, Amy has served up a slice of vlogging reality for both beginners and experienced vloggers that'll help anyone take their online video strategy to the next level. Fun, full of frolics and simply fantastic, this book is one I'll personally refer back to time and time again."

—Chris Ducker, Founder of Youpreneur.com, and Author of *Virtual Freedom*

"Amy is brilliant. They say if you can't explain something to a five-year-old, you don't understand it well enough. Amy breaks down topics in marketing, blogging and video well enough to have a five-year-old vlogging like a boss in no time!"

—Marques Brownlee, YouTuber

"Only fools will try to start a video series without reading this book first. *Vlog Like a Boss* is a perfect mix of inspirational and tactical advice. Highly recommended!"

—Jay Baer, President of Convince & Convert, and Author of *Hug Your Haters*

"If you're not doing online video right now then you're missing a serious opportunity for fame, business exposure, storytelling, or plain old-fashioned connection. Kids (and their parents) all over the world are killing it with video. In this book, YouTube sensation Amy Schmittauer unpacks the precise steps she herself followed to conquer online video so that you can do the same. Amy's a double-threat: fantastic on-camera and just as good at telling you why she is and how you can be, too. Buy this book."

—Matthew Kimberley, Author of *How To Get A Grip*

"Amy's authenticity and passion are inspiring. She makes it easy to learn from her, and I have learned a lot."

—Michelle Tillis Lederman,
Best-Selling Author of *The 11 Laws of Likeability*

"When I need help vlogging, Amy is the first one I contact. She knows her content and communicates it effectively through her proven process. She recently spoke at my conference and the sold-out crowd gave her a standing ovation at the conclusion of her session. Read this book to save time and money and start vlogging like a boss."

—Kary Oberbrunner, Author of *Elixir Project*,
Day Job to Dream Job, *The Deeper Path*,
and *Your Secret Name*

"Simply put, Amy gets video. It is clear that Amy has mastered the art and science of how to leverage video as a powerful marketing vehicle. It's that mastery that has allowed her to generate such a rabid following and positioned her as one of the smartest video marketers in the industry."

—Erik Harbison, CMO for AWeber.com

"Amy combines 9 years of video experience with 30-ish years of being a human into the ultimate resource for anyone looking to start vlogging or any business looking to increase their online presence with video. When it comes to being human in front of a camera, there is no one better than Amy Schmittauer."

—Vincenzo Landino, Creative Director for Aftermarq

"Being able to teach others to vlog is Amy's specialty. She does it with not only knowledgeable tips, but when she tosses in her own personality, humor, and grace, you know you have a winning combination. When looking to start vlogging, Amy is your "boss lady" to give you the most valuable tips to start you out on the right foot. Start reading the book, press record, and click the "publish" button—it's time to VLOG!"

—Stephanie Carls, My Savvy Life on YouTube

"You may think video is scary, and you're right, it is— not because you aren't a good creator or storyteller but because you don't have the toolkit, mindset, and plan that experts like Amy have implemented with extreme success. Amy's ability to create engaging videos that deliver a polished message while being fun has transformed my video creation process. Beyond the social media and equipment advice, Vlog Like A Boss will be your go-to guide as you overcome your fear of video."

—Brian Fanzo,
Global Speaker and Founder of iSocialFanz

"Since I started following Amy, I have been able to create better videos with all of her great tips and tricks. Amy is truly connected with her community which makes it much more effective and genuine. She is always there to help! Thank you, Amy, for being such a rock star!"

—Jean Richer, Vlog Boss University member and
Realtor at Keller Williams Integrity

"If you want to start creating video, then you need to read this book. Amy shares some video tips and tactics to get you creating video straight away."

—Andrew Browne, Vlog Boss University member and IT Consultant at Aussie I.T. Solutions

"*Vlog Like a Boss* takes Amy Schmittauer's insight to a whole new level! Amy's spunky, on-camera personality shines throughout her book, as any loyal Savvy Sexy Social YouTube subscriber would expect. This book is filled with encouragement and inspiration, but most importantly, actionable advice for any level of vlogger."

—Meredith Marsh, Vlog Boss University Member and Founder of VidProMom.com

"Successful athletes never stop strengthening their mindsets and skills. They know victory is not found in their comfort zones, so they seek out winning coaches for a push, proven paths, and encouragement. Successful marketers and communicators do the same. If you want to create impactful and want-to-view videos for your business or organization, *Vlog Like a Boss* is where to start. You won't find a better coach than Amy Schmittauer."

—Tom Page, Vlog Boss University Member and Founder of School Communicators Network

"Amy's videos have been a go-to resource for me over the last few years and will continue to be a guiding light for any of my vlogging, blogging, podcasting, strategy, tactics, and execution in the years to come. *Vlog Like a Boss* is a great addition to the Schmittauer media empire."

—Keith Lewis, Vlog Boss University Member

"*Vlog Like a Boss* is an essential read for anybody wanting to crush it with video. It provides a logical, step-by-step approach to vlogging, but is delivered in a passionate and inspiring way. Writing for the modern world where video can no longer be an overlooked medium, Amy Schmittauer is a true thought leader in the industry, and she holds nothing back in this book to get you vlogging like a boss too."

—Andrew & Pete, Vlog Boss University Members and Co-founders of andrewandpete.com

"Reading this book makes me feel like I'm sitting next to my BFF and listening to her spill it all. Amy's witty, to-the-point voice shines through, reminding me that video is always a good idea, no matter what excuses I'm making that day. The moral of the story is this: do the work, embrace your unique personality, and you'll be vlogging like a boss in no time."

—Amber Rose Monaco, Vlog Boss University Member and writer at The Amber Monaco Creative Content Marketing

"What I've learned from Amy—how to use video to reach more people as a teacher and have greater influence as an authority in my field—has had a huge, immediate impact on my calling as clergy and my career as a community leader. This book is the 100-proof distillation of her years of experience and expertise. If you follow it, you won't be an overnight success—no one is—but you will experience rapid, profound growth in your authority and influence while saving hundreds (or thousands) of hours and dollars in trial and error. Thank you, Amy—my YouTube rabbi!"

—John Carrier, Vlog Boss University Member and Rabbi

How to Kill It Online with
Video Blogging

AMY SCHMITTAUER

AUTHOR ACADEMY elite

Paperback 978-1-946114-16-7

Hardcover 978-1-946114-17-4

Library of Congress Control Number: 2016918820

To my mom, Jacquie.
Thank you for teaching me independence,
work ethic, and focus. More importantly, thank you for
showing me that I can do anything.
I love you.

CONTENTS

Part Three: Kill It Like a Boss

FOREWORD
BY THE SAVVY SEXY SOCIAL COMMUNITY

As I thought about who would be the most appropriate person to write a foreword for this book, I realized it was a no-brainer decision. There is no one on earth that knows me better and can advocate for the work I do more than the community that has been watching my videos for Savvy Sexy Social.

I asked them in a video for words to share with you. Here is what just a few of them said:

Amy Lin 11 hours ago
1) You show me the importance of being yourself, and it is ok to be yourself.
2) You never know when your unique perspective/experience will brighten up someone's day.

Reply · 👍 👎 ♥

Angelique Ridore 20 hours ago
1) Amy's Channel gives you everything you need to be a Brand Boss and she motivated me to Vlog before I ever imagined it was possible that I could be doing it.

2) Video is ubiquitous now and if you have a message, a Brand, or any business...why wouldn't you want a proven no fluff content source to get it done right...the first time!

Reply · 👍 👎

AsPrettyDoes 15 hours ago
What do Amy and Vlogging have in common? They both changed my life! Video gave personality to my business and Amy gave me the push and resources I needed to take both to the next level.

Reply · 👍 👎 ♥

Billy Thompson 16 hours ago
your videos on both schmittastic and on SavvySexySocial has helped me better understand how to best get started by video blogging. now is the best time for people to get started with video blogging to get the most organic reach for not only their personal brands but for any business that they are trying to start.

Reply · 1 👍 👎 ♥

Brian Musial 9 hours ago
You're not a "Hey look at me I made 100k a month as a video-preneur" Douchie McBaggerson.

That's exactly why we need you (Yes YOU reading this) to vlog your story.

Reply · 1 👍 👎 ♥

CoolCat Carolena 9 hours ago
1) You taught me there is always a way to make the video, no excuses, don't quit, my audience wants to hear from me, but it's up to me: MAKE THE VIDEO!
2) Video is for everyone because it's the future - video is education, business development, entertainment, communication - video can be everything or just what YOU need it to be.

Reply · 1 👍 👎 ♥

Christine Morse 17 minutes ago
You have helped me in more ways than I can count but the MAIN way would be that I am just more confident in front of the camera and because of that behind it. I truly believe that if you want to make a difference in your business, your community and the world video is the #1 way to go about doing that.

Reply · 👍 👎 ♥

CraigH JohnsonTC 14 hours ago
Amy taught me the value of getting started, worry about the content and not the equipment. The biggest value in why someone should start blogging is to start building confidence, a vlog can organize your thought leadership and allow you to focus on the skills and experience you do have.

Reply · 👍 👎 ♥

Damian Noud 16 hours ago
Amy's practical tips cut to the chase and gave me the confidence to start vlogging a year ago. Things have snowballed for me since then and anyone who wants to vlog like a boss needs to get on board the Amy train towards their success destination.

Reply · 👍 👎 ♥

David Gonzalez 9 hours ago
Amy, you gave me the courage to find and approach guests for my livestream show unintimidated via the technique used directly from one of your videos. Anyone who has an inkling that they may want to blog or get themselves out there would best serve themselves by learning the lessons from your content and experience.

Reply · 👍 👎 ♥

DHRUV PATEL 11 hours ago
There was always some hesitancy in me from birth but you have helped me to develop my personality. & I think people who face the same challenges should learn and grow from where they are.

Reply · 1 👍 👎 ♥

All Dogs Are Smart 15 hours ago
Amy "encouraged" me to get of my a*@ and vlog already. You should start vlogging because it is the fastest way to get your message out there. Hands down.

Reply · 1 👍 👎 ♥

Doug Neville 16 hours ago

After meeting you in Boston and discussing what I should focus on... I got off my bottom and made some videos! Amy makes getting started super easy, if you don't want to make a video after watching her... you're just lazy!

Reply · 1 👍 👎 ♥

Doug Boulder 13 hours ago

Following Amy's YouTube channel has helped me be a better marketer and has taught me how to create engaging, valuable content. Learning how to vlog teaches marketers principles that apply to every kind of marketing content and how to engage with their target audience.

Reply · 👍 👎 ♥

Ewen Munro 12 hours ago

1) You've helped me realize the potential with vlogging: being able to reach more people and create a business around vlogging.
2) As well as advancing your own business, vlogging can teach you so much about yourself and give you life skills that'll help you in all walks of life.

Reply · 👍 👎 ♥

Family History Fanatics 15 hours ago

1. Amy has helped my family organize, plan, and prepare for another season of vlogging for our niche and pointed out the biggest mistakes to avoid.
2. To improve the quality of niche education, vlogging is an excellent way to achieve that goal and build a personal business as well.
Read more

Reply · 👍 👎 ♥

FitChickGlows 11 hours ago

You encouraged me, informed me, educated me, pulled me up by my bootstraps, and kept me focused on my digital goals 👍! PEEPS wanna KNOW, VIDEO's the way to GO!

Reply · 2 👍 👎 ♥

Haley Hall 7 hours ago

The day I discovered your channel, BAM! I quickly learned from you that video blogging for my business could be silly and educational at the same time. Start vlogging today if you want to establish stronger connections, build your brand, and have fun while doing it.

Reply · 1 👍 👎 ♥

Unruly Housewife 13 hours ago

You have taken the time to write genuine, funny and insightful replies to me - which has encouraged me and made me feel valued (even as a small YouTuber).
Someone should get started with video blogging today, because sharing what you know is too much fun to put off until tomorrow.

Reply · 1 👍 👎 ♥

Jason Kicke 1 hour ago (edited)

Overall, it is your competence that inspires me to achieve my goals. Video blogging "is the most efficient way in which society entertains, educates, shares and communicates with the world."

Reply · 👍 👎 ♥

Jeff Kisler 16 hours ago

You have helped me realize that I don't have any excuses for not doing video and have provided the encouragement I needed to develop and start implement my YouTube strategy for 2017. At the end of the day people have to trust our brand. No other medium does that better than video blogging.

Reply · 1 👍 👎 ♥

Jennifer Southern 18 hours ago

Amy taught me to just get out there and do it(using video), while showing me tools and tricks to look good, while I learn.

Video blogging has been the best way for me to close the distance between myself and my audience, creating an intimate relationship.

Reply · 👍 👎 ♥

thejentennat 16 hours ago

Amy helped me jump into to making videos. She motivates me to just do it and not let my inner critic stop me. I find her videos great sources of knowledge and motivation. 2017 is my year to vlog like a boss.

Reply · 1 👍 👎 ♥

Jessica Smith 13 hours ago

You've helped me begin to get over my fears about video blogging and just do it.

Everyone has a message to share with the world, video blogging is a great way to figure out what your message is and a means with which to share that message.

Reply · 👍 👎 ♥

Jody Yarborough 16 hours ago

1) Amy has helped me have the self-confidence to get over being new to video-blogging and just keep practicing and working harder to get better.
2) I think anyone who has a passion to create and share their perspective should try the video platform. It is one of the most powerful mediums to communicate in today's world.

Reply · 1

Mrs Joyful Jones Vlogs 16 hours ago

Amy explains vlogging in a no nonsense way, she is like a good friend who tells you what's what. Video is best way to get noticed and build a true community.

Reply · 6

Kate's Adventures 12 hours ago

You helped me to think more strategically about my videos and to always strive to improve. I'm motivated to create better content consistently and to think creatively about how my videos can be presented.
Other people should vlog because it's a great way of capturing your life and adventures to share with friends and family... or even to look back on to remember good times!

Reply · 1

Kate Doster 13 hours ago

You're VEDA (Vlogg everyday in april + august) helped me get over my slump with livestreaming. I was able to score a buttload of freelance copywriting clients, just because I was on Periscope just talking about sales copy. It worked so well, I stop live streaming because my wait list was so long. <—That's why you need regular video content people.

Reply ·

ItsKelsiesLife 14 hours ago

Amy's given me countless tips, I ran out and purchased a 35mm lens and a ring light because Amy said so! Treating the camera like a person has been my goal since I started watching her videos, (and after meeting you at SMMW16) I became even more motivated to #vloglikeaboss
If anyone is toying with the idea of video blogging, then DO IT! Amy's made it clear that you may be talking to no one for a while, but the viewers will come if you stay consistent!
Show less

Reply ·

Kezlovesmusic 16 hours ago

You helped me inspire me to make videos and you gave me so many tips on how to constantly get better at video making. Other people should make videos because it can be really fun, life fulfilling and you can discover your very own community.

Reply · 1

Lavontay Santos 14 hours ago

Amy taught me how to truly connect to my audience with nothing but a camera and a story. If you want to make a genuine impact in someone else's life, do two things, listen to Amy, and start video vlogging today.

Reply ·

Lester Suciati 13 hours ago

After 7 years of following Amy on Twitter and 5+ years on YouTube, I knew everything I needed to begin but when to begin, and Amy gave me the knowledge and courage for a beginning. If you want to skip years of research and have the knowledge to start vlogging soonest, follow Amy today.

Read more

Reply ·

lindseys lifeNstyle 5 hours ago

by overcoming my fear of creating you have always taught me to just turn on the camera and press record!

Reply ·

Linue Lee 9 hours ago

Today, right now, your voice matters, because through the internet, you have access to a world of information, people, and tools that can change someone else's life across the world. Amy showed me the power that video has in communicating those meaningful ideas, and in the process, connecting with real people in real ways that help me become better at what I do.

Reply ·

Man after 30 58 minutes ago

It is impossible to mention just one thing that you have helped (like going straight to the point right after video is started) me when I started but now the thing that help me the most is just that you are the great example of how you have changed in a good way during these years just by doing more and this is what I strongly admire.
Why others should start video bloging is because this is the best way to get out of comfort zone, to meet new people and opportunities and to improve yourself in so many ways that it is really hard to imagine.
Show less

Reply ·

Marie Helene D. 19 hours ago
I've done one of Amy's courses on how to start vlogging for business and it was a game changer for me. No doubt for me that video is one of the most powerful tools to grow your business and build your authority.
So, thank you Amy :-)

Reply · 👍 🏴 ♥

Mark LeMaster 13 hours ago (edited)
1. I was honored to meet you at the Igniting Souls Conference in Columbus, OH, where you helped me by challenging me (and the entire audience) to participate in creating my first "horrible" video!
2. I am now on Day 24 of your "30 Days to Better Vlogging" and have referred several of my friends to this course because it is powerful and practical material that doesn't leave me overwhelmed!

Reply · 👍 🏴 ♥

MJSiebolt By Matthew J S Dykstra 8 hours ago
Matthew Dykstra "MJSiebolt": You have helped me so much by teaching me the best ways to vlog and personally checking my site and replying back what you thought. I think video is the way to go just having a blog like a book is okay but people want media and you can help them by learning how to create the best you can.

Reply · 👍 🏴 ♥

Meg Oh-Kay 14 hours ago
I have recently joined the freelance lifestyle and I credit Amy's advice with giving me the confidence I have to keep going after what I want. If you are looking for a no fluff, real take on how to make your side hustle your breadwinner, Amy is for you!

Reply · 👍 🏴 ♥

Michal Krzak 30 minutes ago
I came across Amy's video blog when I was looking for some video shooting tips to promote my wife's interior design company. I started watching Amy's videos one after another and then something magical happened - it pushed me to start my own content marketing company. So it was even more important to me than starting a video blog (which by the way starts at the beginning of 2017). I believe that you should give it a try and build your dream.

Reply · 👍 🏴 ♥

Sal Coombes 1 day ago (edited)
I follow a #Shit Ton of social media experts. No one explains things as well, as real, as relatable as Amy. She's RIGHT about everything.
Amy will save you from doing stupid things on social media. The outcome, you'll do more of what actually works.

Reply · ·

Samantha Melanie 16 hours ago
Amy, you've taught me so much about how YouTube actually works & how grow a channel, in your classic honest, mildly sarcastic, & no b*llshit wine drinking fashion! ♥

People should start vlogging because everyone has an interest or a passion- why not pick up a camera and share it with the rest of the world?! 🐸
Show less

Reply · 1 👍 🏴 ♥

SaraMakerAlt 16 hours ago (edited)
Amy has helped me by convincing me of the power of video in the first place. Video really lets people feel like they know you more than text does, since they can see and hear you.

Reply · 1 👍 🏴 ♥

slipshift 20 hours ago
Amy helped me understand many of the best practices to engaging with a community.
If you want to start, you are just wasting time.

Reply · · ·

Some Things About Her 9 hours ago
You have helped me understand the missing pieces from my vlog. I'm still working on 30 days to a better blog and I know that I will have more details after the course is over.
Someone should start video blogging to reach people they may not reach in a traditional settings.

Reply · 👍 🏴 ♥

StephCitGhosts 6 hours ago
You helped me realize that I was good enough, because of you I was able to look past my self criticism and start my channel that has become a huge part of my life. Video blogging is not only enjoyable and very therapeutic, but also a way to record memories for yourself, not only the viewers.

Reply · 👍 🏴 ♥

The Redesign 15 hours ago
Who knew that opening up to the realm of video blogging could help an audio only podcast...Amy; it expanded my podcast listenership to an audience who wouldn't have even known I existed. The world of video not only increases exposure to your brand but it also allows listeners/followers/fans to see a more up close and real version of you.

Reply ·

Tony Thomas 14 hours ago
You have helped me to realize the power of personalized video communication and its ability to easily reach and influence thousands of people via YouTube. I think others should read your book to be able to actualize this tremendous potential to build their brand.

Reply ·

Vince Lia 5 hours ago (edited)
Your 30 Days to Better Vlogging Guide is a tool bag full of tips and tricks that I often refer back to when I need inspiration or want to improve on an aspect of my video content that you've discussed. Everyone should invest in vlogging to reveal a more personal side of their lives to the viewer and create a deeper connection with their audience.

Reply ·

I am humbled by this community's response and continually blown away by the power of video. Thank you, Socials.

INTRODUCTION

My hands gripped the steering wheel. Alone in the car, enthusiastically dancing to the song on the radio, I was pretty sure anyone driving next to me was watching. I'd been on the road for about two hours headed to a destination that was only five minutes from my home.

It was a gorgeous fall day and I was spending the weekend in Hocking Hills with friends, thus the drive time. I had agreed to go on the trip before I knew I would need to be home—in Downtown Columbus, Ohio—that same weekend for a once-in-a-lifetime, ten-minute appointment.

I was going to drive Gary Vaynerchuk to the airport.

A) No, I'm not crazy. B) No, I'm not a stalker. C) Yes, this was a Very Big Deal.

Here's the gist:

Gary Vaynerchuk is a marketing and business icon. He's the guy who totally gets this online influence phenomenon we're currently living in, teaching his clients of Vaynermedia as well as the online world how seriously they should be taking it too.

Gary has a book launch ritual. He hosts an eight-hour promotional live video stream whenever he has a new book coming out. Taking questions from the chat participants (sometimes without a bathroom break for the entire eight hours), he makes a connection with his community throughout the Q&A while further encouraging book sales. Some of those lucky people tuning in will get picked to come on-screen and ask a video question live.

As a viewer of this stream in 2013, I somehow got to be one of the lucky few to go live and ask a video question directly to @GaryVee himself.

Whatever the question was, it was totally brilliant. Gary was impressed. My ego was stroked. I felt pretty good about myself.

Then he posed a question to me, "How many books are you buying?"

I used the opportunity to negotiate a shot at a meeting in return for what he felt was an appropriate bulk book buy (say that 3x fast). This resulted in a conversation about his upcoming Columbus trip and need for airport transportation.

Hence my role as his one-way ticket from a downtown Columbus hotel to Columbus International Airport. (Shout-out to Janine Sickmeyer. She went in on the buy with me so she could assist with the other half of his transportation coming into town. #RoundTripGirlPower #WinWinWin)

While my friends in Hocking Hills went on a hiking adventure, I set off in my boyfriend's car (which I had to borrow because I didn't even own a car). I had hours to plan exactly how I would redeem my ten minutes of one-on-one time with the man who would become one of the greatest digital mentors of this stage of my career.

I nervously approached the familiar Crowne Plaza down the street from where I lived. A little early, so right on time.

I parked in a back alley where I knew I could sit for a moment without trouble and waited. I peered at the hotel doors. No one but valet staff in sight.

A text pinged my phone. It was *the* Gary Vaynerchuk. Texting my phone number. Is this even happening?! What is life right now?

"Ready when you are." Straight to the point.

I replied, "Parked outside!"

I put my hazard lights on in the illegal parking spot and got out of the car. Walking just a few steps over to the hotel doors, I saw a man in a hoodie and jeans, phone clutched in one hand and the other dragging a small roller bag. There he was. I smiled so he would know it was me.

"Mr. Vaynerchuk, it's so nice to finally meet you," I stretched out my hand for a shake which he did not accept, leaning in for a hug instead.

The Scale of Moments

It sounds like it could have been awkward, right? Do you shake hands or do you hug? As you debate, the other person decides to move in, and you end up in this total guy hug (whether you're a guy or not) like you're afraid to look too excited or be accepting of germs. It makes you hate yourself a little and wish you would have just been the gutsy one to offer an embrace in the first place. But you didn't. So you are the one who made it weird.

Except it wasn't weird. It was great. As half-way or accidental as it may have ended up, it completely knocked down the walls of nervousness and started an incredible new friendship right then and there. (I mean, after an awkward hug like that we're totally friends now, right?)

That was the first *moment* for me. That was the moment when a little lady in her twenties who had been running her first business alone for almost three years started to realize that it doesn't have to be all about business all the time.

Gary put his bag in the back and then jumped into the passenger seat. I returned to gripping the steering wheel and started to realize what I had signed up for.

I was about to operate a motor vehicle on the freeway with the beloved Gary Vaynerchuk in the front seat. The nerves came back. This time accompanied by an immense feeling of responsibility.

He put on his seatbelt. Smart.

After I had reminded myself of how many books I'd bought in the negotiation, I decided to go through with it instead of calling Uber to my rescue. (Just kidding. Columbus didn't have Uber until December of that year. Thus, Gary's need for a ride.)

I shifted the car into drive as Gary did a final check of his phone and then switched it off and dove in.

"Okay, so tell me what you're working on." I handed him my dark purple business card for my YouTube channel, Savvy Sexy Social, which I had in the ready position on the dashboard. I began explaining what I do and how the YouTube channel helps me promote that business. Then, before I could finish—

"I've already seen this," he said. "I looked up your content, and you do really good work. What is your business model and how can I help?"

He looked me up? Sorry, wut? Can you repeat that?

Gary Vaynerchuk went to my channel and potentially, maybe, could have pressed play on a video?

R u 4 real?

This was a mind-blowing concept to me. I was stunned. I may have wasted a whole 30 seconds of the drive just in processing time. (Get it? Processing time?)

This was Moment #2. Only three minutes later reconfirming that people in business can be cool people. What. Is. Happening?!

I went on to multitask: merging onto the freeway and not killing Gary Vaynerchuk via motor vehicle accident, while explaining my business ideas for video in the social media space.

Gary provided a lot of great insight on the fly from his experience. It was exactly what I needed to better understand what I was getting myself into. Money's worth like whoa.

Remember how I said I was getting ten minutes with Gary? Let me correct myself. The airport is about seven minutes from Downtown. Yes, the ride was basically over when it started.

Before I knew it, we had safely arrived at Port Columbus as I pulled into passenger drop-off, thanking Gary and then hugging him goodbye for now (this time, awkward-driver-seat hug).

Grateful, I promised to review his book for my YouTube audience once I'd received it in the mail. (The book was still in pre-launch and had yet to hit Amazon officially.) He thanked me, grabbed his bag, waved back, and then headed into the terminal. I started my drive back to Hocking Hills.

In the Spirit

A short time later, I received the shipment of books I'd ordered upon the title's public release. *Jab, Jab, Jab, Right Hook* would go on to become a New York Times Best Seller (obviously…the guy knows how to hustle for book sales if you haven't noticed). I was ready to crack it open and read it cover-to-cover to make good on posting a review for my community.

I love reading the books written by my friends and colleagues as much as I like to read from people I don't actually know. They spent all this time and energy to write on a subject they've become an expert in to compile a 300-page baby. I love to support that! And learn something new in the process.

But this practice sometimes results in reading some pretty subpar books. No disrespect to anyone for their very hard work writing a book. Quite frankly, you might feel this way about what you're reading right now. I'm okay with that.

When I read *Jab, Jab, Jab, Right Hook*, I was over the moon about how good it was. This isn't a book. It is *the* manual for social media success. *And* it has pictures.

This was something the industry desperately needed, and it was exactly what I wanted all of my community to read before they posted any status updates or shared a blog or vlog with their followers. Ever. Again.

When I finished it, I couldn't wait to film my review. I was so pumped to sit in front of my handy Canon Powershot and rave about the pages I'd read. "You must buy this and keep it on your desk!" I would say.

The book came out late in the year, and I'm a pretty spirited girl during the holidays. Yes, I *am* the overly cheery girl listening to the Christmas Spotify playlist soon after Halloween. We all have our happy place, okay?

While spreading my usual cheer one Sunday, driving home from the grocery store, I was listening to the local holiday station. My all-time favorite Christmas song came on: the massively successful and beloved "All I Want for Christmas is You" by Mariah Carey.

(Fun fact: did you know Mariah didn't even want to do a Christmas album because she was worried about what it would do for her image? Thank Santa someone changed her mind about that.)

I started singing along, as one does. (Funny how we're already back to a singing-in-the-car moment, by the way.) Sometimes I get bored of the lyrics I already know and start to make up my own. When I tried to pull new words out of my brain this time, out of nowhere, I started replacing the chorus, "All I want for Christmas is *you!*" with, "All I want for Christmas is *Jab, Jab, Jab, Right Hooooooook!*"

It was weird, but it worked. The melody landed in place with the beat, and so I tried to nail it down again.

Throughout the verses, I tried to keep with the theme, coming up with ideas that I'd read in Gary's best seller and improvising whatever I could into the proper syllables of the song. It was working. Way, way, way too well.

I couldn't let it go. I didn't even unpack groceries before sitting down at home, reviewing the song on repeat, and flipping through the book to nail down a parody version of the holiday hit. I wrote my entire version on paper within a half hour.

The song stuck in my head. I grabbed my MacBook Air and Blue Snowball microphone to go into the closet for a more ~~hidden~~ sound-controlled space. I opened the app GarageBand for the first time and tinkered around to figure out how to use it to record vocals. I was used to video editors, but audio looked like a very different spaceship. I eventually had the minimum knowledge required to lay down some music.

Using a copyright-free re-creation of the background track for Mariah's song (thank you, YouTube musicians), I started to sing the lyrics into the microphone.

Can we just pause to consider the ridiculousness that is happening here?

Marketing consultant.

In her bedroom closet.

Singing at the top of her lungs to sound somewhat in tune with Mariah Carey, using parody-style lyrics about a social media book.

Really take that in.

Now, think about how weird it was to hear your own voice talking into a tape recorder (for the millennial+ crowd out there) or your voice memo app for the first time. How about the time you watched yourself in a video?

Cringe-worthy doesn't even do it justice, right?

Now, feel all those feels for every lyric of that song that I had to sing, go back, listen to, and redo or approve. Line-by-line from my mediocre-at-best audio equipment with my subpar Mariah Carey impersonation.

Painful. Anxiety-building. Vomit-inducing. You get the idea.

Anyway, the song was *done*, and that was enough adventure for one day. Tomorrow I would get camera-ready and film myself dancing along to the track to complete my utterly absurd and risky first-ever musical book review to upload to YouTube.

The Big Reveal

The video was finally ready. It was time for me to change the settings on the YouTube upload from private to public. Well, except for the fact that YouTube was pretty darn sure I *was* Mariah Carey (Really, YouTube? Really?), which meant I would not be able to monetize the video with ads while it was under further review.

"Oh well. That's not why I made this thing anyway." I shared the video. It was live. *Gulp.*

I started checking my email like any other day at the office, but I couldn't get my mind off what I had just done.

I was checking for tweets and YouTube comments every few minutes.

I decided I would email Gary to let him know how much I loved the book and that I did something kinda different for the review. (Kinda different? Girl, you fell off the deep end.) I shared a link to the video and alluded to him watching it if he had the time.

I don't know what happened to that particular piece of correspondence. Although I sent it, later I would discover how it didn't end up mattering at all.

When I found out that Gary was doing a live interview that morning with Chase Jarvis on Creative Live, I watched. I wanted to figure out when he would be looking at Twitter again, something he does religiously to stay engaged and in-the-know with his community.

Maybe he would see that I copied him on my tweet about the video, and he would click the image of his book in my hands. Would that be enough when the whole world was reviewing his book right now? Especially after an interview with a huge new audience on a popular live stream?

But a funny thing happened throughout the time Gary was in that interview. People were watching my video and tweeting Gary. They weren't just sharing the video and copying both of us on the tweets. They were wildly clamoring for Gary to see it.

Tweets like "Have you seen this?" and "OMG @Gary-Vee" flooded his Twitter timeline, enough to be peppered in with the Creative Live tweets and draw a little attention as a blip on his radar.

The interview ended. Gary started checking tweets. I watched his profile and saw him begin to reply to people.

"@coolperson1234 thanks"

"@fabulousfriend9876 awesome"

"@supertweeter5678 ;)"

Quick replies to as many people as possible who had tuned into his interview. I watched them all come in.

I might have to take that not-a-stalker promise back.

And then, suddenly, the replies stopped. For a minute. Then two. Then when it got closer to four minutes, I knew he had seen it. He was watching my video right now. I could feel it.

Sure enough, there it was. His next tweet.

"OMG!!!!!! This is incredible Please watch this!" Followed by a link to my YouTube video. 3:25pm ET December 3, 2013.

He didn't stop there. He posted it on his Facebook fan page as well.

Oh. My. *God.*

Moment #3. People are cool. Even in business. Cool enough, even when they're well-known, that they are as overwhelmed by your generosity as you are of theirs.

I'm not sure what moment-number my music video was for Gary, but I know it ranked on his scale. Finding your way onto someone's scale of moments is what I believe the trick to this whole thing is. Incredibly, it all goes back to being human and showing appreciation—giving value and not expecting anything in return.

This musical book review has grown to more than 15,000 YouTube views. This is nowhere near the top of the list of highest-viewed content on my channel of over 650 videos. However, it is one video that I can credit for hundreds of YouTube subscribers, tons of new friendships, almost 100 client inquiries, and thousands of dollars in products sold.

The increase to the bottom line is one big reason so many people are trying to learn how to be more human on the internet. More incredible, though, is when you have this eye-opening and groundbreaking moment, when suddenly money is of little importance compared to the achievement of having amazing people enter your life. Since that video, Gary has released another book, of which I received an advance copy and a personal request from Mr. Vaynerchuk himself for another musical book review, which I did just a few months ago.

Jab Jab Jab Right Hook: A Musical Book Review (http://savvysexysocial.com/JJJRH) was episode 205 of Savvy Sexy Social. It wasn't how I got my start because technically I'd had a lot of experience in video at that point. But at the same time, it felt like an incredible beginning.

To get the attention I wanted, I had to do things I wasn't comfortable with. I had to be vulnerable. I had to take a chance. I had to let imperfection go live on the internet. I had to focus on making something great for one person to help the many.

I did the *work*.

Most importantly, I did the *work*.

There's something you should know before you read this book: I'm not just another motivational-hype-woman for the internet. I don't sit around and think about the possibilities of what could happen with social video and then blog about it as if I had real experience.

I am *doing* this stuff. I am in the trenches finding out what works, when, and for who. "Practical" is my name and "execution" is my game. I don't know any other way.

Vlog Like a Boss is for go-getters and creators. It's for those who go after what they want in life and want to kill it online.

So if you didn't pick up this book with the intention to get stuff done, it's not your time to vlog like a boss. I've taken everything I've learned over the years and compiled it into this no-nonsense, comprehensive guide so that you can get started immediately.

You may not totally understand the world of video right now. It might even scare you. But that shouldn't be what holds you back. I want you to take a chance with me to see what you're capable of. Because when I say, "If I can do it, you can too," it's absolutely true.

The key is to focus on what makes *you* great and keep doing the work. This pairing will be astronomically more productive than staying inside your comfort zone. My hope is that you will have just one moment that ranks on your scale so you start to see how big this could be.

Let's dive in.

PART ONE
LAUNCH LIKE A BOSS

CHAPTER ONE
WHAT'S A VLOG?

Vlogging. What a funny word.

Even funnier might be why you're here reading this book. Maybe you've watched a few great online videos (or more than a few...I see you, YouTube lovers) and thought about sharing your story with a camera. Maybe you're being pressured to think about video blogging because of the changing landscape of reaching people online.

Maybe you're just lonely—no reason to be ashamed of that. It's how many people have stumbled into a career on YouTube.

What is a vlog? Let's break this down.

Vlog
[vlawg, vlog]
noun
1.   a blog that features mostly videos rather than text or images.
(credit: dictionary.com)

The word "blog" is something we're all pretty familiar with these days. Blog is a short version of "weblog." You're logging stories, experiences, advice, or anything else through content on the web when you blog.

To vlog, essentially, is to add a video component to that. So rather than a weblog, it's a video weblog or video blog. Shortened, we get the word *vlog*.

When I think about a vlog, I think of any online content that is documented and shared through video. A vlog and a video blog are the same thing in my opinion.

I also want you to know how committed I am to this book right now. My iMac, which I'm currently writing on, absolutely refuses to stop autocorrecting vlog to blog. Could I fix it somehow? Probably. Have I figured that out? No. I'm too busy writing a book.

Quite simply, you should think of a vlog as video content you're sharing to communicate with an audience online.

You're looking into the eyes of your viewers when you talk to a camera. You understand them. You help them. You relate to them. That is all vlogging is. It's being human on camera.

Why would you choose video in the first place, much less video blogging? This isn't a decision many take lightly, so what does it mean for you to use this platform to achieve your goals when you could go with so many other options?

Vlogging and YouTube

Although I will be commenting on many video-friendly social platforms throughout this book, a heavy focus will be on YouTube and the whys and hows of working with this network. Not only is it where I got my start, but it's still the reigning champion for video online. Facebook, Instagram, and Snapchat are starting to change that dynamic, but the relevancy and attention paid to the kingpin of online video is far too important to ignore.

The key here is *searchability*. If you're doing it well, search results are going to generate the majority of your inbound video traffic. When we think of search results, we think of Google. ("Unless you're reading this far into the future when Bing finally takes over," *said no one ever*.)

Google is the coveted search engine for anyone who wants their online content to be discovered, which is what makes YouTube so powerful as well. YouTube started as the shiny new video-sharing platform in February 2005, but then Google acquired it in late 2006 making it the powerhouse we know now. These are the #1 and #2 search engines on the internet today, YouTube following its adopted mommy, Google.

Visual learners go to YouTube first to find what they need to know. But when anyone goes to Google, YouTube results also appear. You are using both search engines at once, getting you the best results every time. Thus, the best search resource ever.

Leveraging video to share your message is such an advantage that those who integrate video into a blog post on their website are 53 times more likely to appear on the front page of a relevant Google search (credit: Forrester Research). More on this later.

Let's talk about the less data-oriented reason that video is critical for building brand awareness. The reality is that in the world of social media, everyone can be your peer. Meaning, we're all on a level playing ground when we engage an online audience. Susie Teenager tweeting her thumbs off has the same potential to make an impact as Coca-Cola. No matter who you are, you're going to be challenged if you want to stand out from all the noise.

The benefit of video is that you can make that connection as quickly as pressing the record button. You'll start to build rapport, trust, and authority immediately upon sharing a video full of your ideas. This is your opportunity to sit down with thousands of people over a cup of coffee (without spending your life savings on lattes).

Being the main feature of your videos can sound daunting. I understand that. We are going to talk about this more coming up.

Do you know what makes vlogging special? It's the people who put themselves out there and become vulnerable. When you choose to make a connection with your face, it's such a bold move—even in today's fairly narcissistic society—that it automatically moves you further ahead. Just making videos isn't enough, but it's a huge first step to standing out.

As we start to think about the fears of creating video and how to overcome them, I think it's only right that you get a glimpse of what it was like to make my first video ever.

CHAPTER TWO
MY FIRST VIDEO

In 2007, one of my best friends from high school called me and asked me to be in her wedding. Nice, right? Well, we were best friends in high school but had not connected much now that we'd moved on to college and adulthood. Let's just say I wasn't the first person she called.

Okay. I was quite literally the last person she called.

See, there was a bridal party of eight (yes, eight ladies) that had been lined up for the big day. The last bridesmaid said yes before becoming pregnant and ended up backing out due to not being able to fit into the dress or do bridesmaid-y things when the time came. I was invited to fill her place.

Since Stephanie was a dear friend to me in high school, I said yes. I also had mad respect for someone lucky enough to have eight amazing people in her life to make up a bridal party that almost resembled a bright pink Dream Team and even afforded the opportunity for an Olympic-like alternate.

I was her Olympic alternate. That's hard to turn down.

This was my first adventure as a bridesmaid, so I wanted to make the most of it. Being the last bridesmaid, both in line and in order of request, I decided I wanted to do something that made me her favorite bridesmaid. A little catty. I know. But I'm competitive like that.

At first, it was super easy. I might have been the last bridesmaid, but I was the first one to get fitted and buy the dress. Stephanie couldn't believe that I took it so seriously. I couldn't believe it either. I was on a mission.

I then teamed up with another bridesmaid and dear friend from high school, Annie. We came up with the idea to do something cool at the rehearsal dinner.

We started to brainstorm what to do, and somehow the harebrained idea to create a video came up. Neither of us had ever made a video, nor had we operated video editing software. What else did we have to do that summer?

A Lesson Learned in Time

I remembered that my Canon Powershot, the go-to vacation camera and selfie tool of 2007, had a video option. We tested it, and it worked! We now knew we had something to create a video with and just needed to figure out what the content would be.

Since we went to school together, the natural thought was to try to find our friends from way back in the day (four years was a lot of time to us back then) and record clips of them wishing Stephanie and her groom well.

On a few occasions, we went back to our hometown of Worthington to knock on doors of people who might be home from college for the summer. We even texted and tracked people down at work.

The most fun times were when we ran into people at the bar. It was already kinda weird running into people we hadn't seen in years, but we had also just reached drinking age. That made everything much weirder. However, the need to talk to someone who never gave you the time of day in high school and approaching them to ask them for a favor of recording them on camera made alcohol a pretty handy partner. #InflatedSelfEsteem

Eventually, we had a nice little compilation of clips. I pressed the power button on my enormous Windows desktop computer that took up half my kitchen and hunted around for an application I remembered seeing when I first purchased the machine.

There it was! Windows Movie Maker.

I pulled all the clips together on the editing timeline following a nice intro sequence of photos from our old neighborhood and school memories, transitioned perfectly with (the totally illegal use of) the heartstring-tugging melody "Good Riddance" by Green Day.

I was proud. I felt like I made something. "It was so easy, and yet no one is doing this," I thought.

When I had finally perfected my editing work and it was time to go to the rehearsal dinner, I burned that video to a DVD and requested some air time while everyone was eating. The organizers needed to hunt around for a tube television with a DVD player attached, but they found it and wheeled it on a cart to the front of the room.

Now that I think about it, this may have been my first speaking experience ever. I don't remember being nervous in the least as we walked up to that television to unveil our surprise for the bride.

"Stephanie, we wanted you to feel even more special on your special day. This is for you."

I pressed play.

We walked to the back of the room and off to the side to watch our work come to life. It immediately felt so different from watching it back in our editing suite. My heart was racing. My eyes were darting around the room. I was praying that the DVD wouldn't skip or any other technical issues arise.

We stood there in a happily nervous state and observed the bride enjoying the intro song and the photos from back in the day. Small steps to get the emotions flowing.

When the personalized video messages began to play and Stephanie saw the faces of old friends in their 2007 bodies, the emotions came pouring out of her. How kind that these people took moments out of their lives to wish her well! How could this be happening?

Watching Stephanie was enough to make you smile for a lifetime. Certainly, it was enough to become the *favorite* bridesmaid.

That first video wouldn't have made the difference in my life if I had just looked at Stephanie. I looked at everyone else in the room. Family, close and distant. Friends and their significant others. The groom's side.

Everyone was so emotional.

It didn't matter if you knew every face on that screen that popped up to say "best wishes." The story that the video told was enough to jerk the tears of nearly anyone. With Stephanie practically balling her eyes out and everyone going through this journey with her, it was the most important moment of my life.

I had created something that mattered. I had the emotions of an entire room of people in the palm of my hand. Simply by pressing play on a piece of work created for one person.

The power in that feeling is extraordinary, and at 21 years old, I'd found my calling.

It felt like a super-fulfilling hobby at the time because I had zero clues about how to make it a career, but just knowing what I was capable of was life-changing. Before that, I hadn't known what I wanted to be when I grew up, but I finally had the sense of relief that I'd been searching for.

"Oh good. I found something."

CHAPTER THREE
THE THREE FEARS

My first video had very little of me on camera and involved more technical discomfort than anything else. "Learner's curve" doesn't even begin to do it justice.

Eventually, I became the subject of 90% of the videos I created. As the adventure continued, there was quite a bit more to attack regarding fears.

Video is scary.

It's vulnerable.

It's weird.

So weird.

If you can get past all of that, you can make bigger moves in this world than you could ever imagine, for the same reason TV and movie stars have so much influence and impact on the average person. They've touched us in some way thanks to the scalability of their talent through video.

You don't have to want to be famous to leverage the vlog, but you do have to have a purpose in your message. Is it important enough to share? So important that you would be willing to break down your fears of video to share that message in a way that would set you apart from the noise?

If that answer is yes, then let's start breaking down those fears now so we can start to make this vlog thing happen for you.

Let's start with my favorite fear, and the one I hear about the most:

The Fear of Gear

You want your videos to be excellent, so your first instinct is to have the nicest equipment to get the job done beautifully.

But, then what?

You're just getting started with video, so that means you need to go out and spend thousands of dollars on the best kit? It's not realistic. Nor is it encouraging.

Because this is the natural instinct of newbies, video never gets created. Thus, the fear of gear. "We don't have the right stuff to get it done, but when we do...."

Yeah. I've heard that one before.

We live in a world in which we can create beautiful content just by pulling our smartphones out of our pockets. You don't even question it when something is going on around you: your child taking her first steps, the dog doing a funny trick, your favorite band playing at the local venue when you're in those prime seats. Smartphone video is the perfect option in these cases.

When it's time to think about your brand awareness plan and video production, though, you stop short at the thought of a phone being your tool of choice. It just doesn't make any sense. Why are you doing that to yourself?

"Do what you can, with what you have, where you are." Theodore Roosevelt. Brilliant. Incredible vlogger. (jk)

The most successful people do whatever they can with what they have, make the most of it, and then upgrade when the time comes. You don't have to have the best gear right now to share your message! Every day you postpone, you're falling further behind.

Your smartphone is powerful. It's one of the most sophisticated cameras ever created. Let's put this in perspective.

The United States put a man on the moon. One of the most incredible achievements in human history.

We take it for granted. Think about this—we put a man in a tin can and sent him to the moon, and he danced around up there while streaming it to the world.

That's unbelievable!

That was in 1969.

I'm not sure if you're an aerospace nerd or not, but you don't need to be. I'm definitely not. Even the nerds probably haven't looked up what technology we were dealing with to achieve such an incredible task.

The Apollo Guidance Computer helped make this whole thing happen. You'll never believe the specs on this thing:

- Processor Speed: 1 MHz
- Memory: 2,048 words (about 4kB)
- Display: Save-Segment Numeric
- Weight: 70 lbs.
- Price: $150,000
- Camera: *Nope*

This is laughable at best. We seriously put a man on the moon guided by this device that's just a few steps away from an overpriced Tinker Toy.

Can you imagine $150,000 in 1969, for a 70-pound computer?

The state of devices back then was interesting enough, but they're even more incredible now because of how far we've come.

Keeping the Apollo computer in mind, let's take a look at a popular smartphone today—the Apple iPhone 7:

- Processor Speed: A10 fusion chip with 64-bit architecture
- Memory: 32-256 GB storage
- Display: 4.7-inch retina HD LED-backlit widescreen
- Weight: 4.87 ounces
- Price: starting at $649
- Camera: 12-megapixel camera with 4K video recording (30 frames per second) and 1080p HD video recording (30 or 60 frames per second)

The little guy in your pocket is an incredibly complex and wonderful device, isn't it? Who says smartphone video isn't good enough?

When I finally launched Savvy Sexy Social, I used the Flip camera, but it was just not what I needed. (Apparently, everyone else felt the same, because they've been discontinued and are now only found on eBay.) I couldn't see myself to make sure I was in the frame. The lens was not wide angle, so the camera had to be very far away to get a decent picture of my upper body. Oh and then that's an audio issue when you're not close enough, right? Yeah, it wasn't my favorite.

But it didn't stop me. I just kept going until I could get the camera I wanted. I proved to myself that I needed it before I made the jump. I executed first so I could feel the pain of that need, not just make it up in my mind. That's the best time to buy a product you know you're going to get your money's worth on. Make yourself feel pained without it on a regular basis because of how much easier it would make your life if you did have it.

When that time came, I still didn't have the budget for a $1,000 camera. I went back to my trusty Canon Power-shot. This time, I purchased one with a larger body and a flip display so I could film myself while knowing exactly how much of the room and my head was in sight.

I used that device for quite some time. The idea of having to buy a fancy camera that I would have to learn how to focus properly and get all in-the-know tech-wise made me want to curl up into a ball. I had work to do. There wasn't time for that! I just wanted to say my piece on this good-enough-camera, edit the video, upload, and move on.

It was also a sense of responsibility for me. Here I was, on my YouTube channel, encouraging small businesses to get social and make video with whatever they had available. How was I supposed to drive that point home while sitting on my high horse of fancy gear?

Then my dear YouTube friend and tech review expert Austin Evans created a video with me at Vidcon in August 2013

> You don't build a portfolio and a career of over 1,000 videos waiting for conditions to be perfect.

about how to get started with video blogging on a DSLR camera. (Check out episode 155.) I used the opportunity to create something useful for my audience, but also to have my friend teach me what to do if I were to finally make the jump to a nicer piece of equipment.

The DSLR video and the following upgrade of the equipment on my channel happened two and a half years after I started it. That's four and a half years after I started making video at all on YouTube.

You don't build a portfolio and a career of over 1,000 videos waiting for conditions to be perfect.

I often read comments from viewers that say something like, "I was so nervous to get started with creating video...and then I watched the first videos you made. Totally feeling better about myself." Now, I could feel super embarrassed when I hear that, but it makes me genuinely happy.

The fact that I had to start somewhere made someone feel empowered enough to get started themselves. Since I have a business model that revolves around helping people create video, that's a win for me.

If your audience feels closer to you by being part of your journey, that's a win for you no matter what you teach or sell.

Your default smartphone camera has quite literally 100x the options I had when I got started. *"When I was your age...."*

This is why Snapchat is so wildly successful. There's not a lot of opportunity for smoke and mirrors. No green screens and editing. You're using your smartphone, or you're not using Snapchat. (At least that's how it is today... who knows what's to come in this ever-changing landscape.) Users love this because they can watch a truly raw experience from their friends and family, and this carries over into businesses and brand names as well. They love to see what it's really like on the other side.

The Fear of Gear is totally valid but, at the same time, it's the excuse before all the other excuses. We will be covering vlogging gear in Chapter Eleven so that you can decide what tools to use as you get started with video, but in my experience, equipment is usually the fear people use as an excuse for this next issue.

The Fear of Personality

I know what you're thinking: video people have been natural on camera all their lives. They were born this way.

But, it's not true. Ask my mom. If there ever was a camera in the vicinity of my face growing up, I was as far away from it as possible.

I was not a ham. I was just trying to get through life one day at a time and make sure I didn't screw up along the way. I was very unsure of myself. I didn't even know how to feel comfortable being myself. Today everyone talks about authenticity. Growing up, being yourself was not so sexy.

My sister was the ham. The photogenic one. The cheerleader. All those things I detested growing up as the awkward older sister. Don't get me wrong. I love my sister. Now. But I had to grow up to realize that.

My point is that she was the one you would have predicted to be the "personality" based on the stereotype of people who love the camera. Then God blessed us with YouTube and that entire argument was drilled straight into the ground.

If you've ever met a YouTube entertainer in real life and seen what the average person making videos in their bedroom is like face-to-face, you know what I'm saying. Sometimes it doesn't quite match up.

But I digress.

How I got my start with video had nothing to do with being a ham or loving the camera or being a natural. Because I wasn't…and I didn't…and I definitely wasn't. It had everything to do with wanting to be the favorite bridesmaid and, even more importantly, having a message worth sharing.

I'm writing this in my early thirties, and even though I'm a little in denial about how quickly time flies, I'm so grateful to be at this moment in my life. Over the last couple of years, I've felt like I finally have permission to be myself. Something just clicked—there was no way I could be a success if I were to be a censored, "acceptable" version of myself.

Let me ask you this right now (because it might be the most important turning point for you to take a chance on video): do you feel like you can and do represent an authentic version of who you are?

It might sound like a big philosophical question, but it's a critical one if you are going to vlog like a boss. Your personality is the only one you get, but it's also the only one you need. You don't have to be like someone else, sound like a success-

> Your personality is the only one you get, but it's also the only one you need.

ful person, or try to find ways to change yourself to fall in line. You gotta be you, or this is *never* going to work.

The rest of this book is going to focus on the technical side of creating the vlog, but you have to feel it in your heart. A massive piece of that equation is you being the human you know how to be. You have my permission to be yourself.

Are you ready for that?

It's not a question of whether your personality is good enough. It's whether you are ready to share it with the world.

Your personality is five percent of this gig. I promise you it's good enough to attack the enormous task of obtaining the talent you need to achieve your vlogging goals. Don't let it hold you back anymore because you have other important work to do.

Talent in video is something you can work on and achieve. The active word here being *work*. It's going to take a lot of planning and execution on your part, but it's worth it, and it's possible.

How do you achieve that talent so you can get better at video and have a vlog worth watching? We will go into great detail on this in Chapter Five. Get ready.

Now that you're not worried about equipment and you're ready to share your amazing personality, let's attack something that might still be bothering you.

The Fear of ROI

Certainly one of the largest fallacies about social media is that you cannot measure return on investment (ROI). It's a laughable concept that somehow by switching to digital forms of communication we would lose any features of measurement.

Have we truly ever been able to measure word of mouth before? Maybe with that paper mailing list on the checkout counter in your local market asking how you heard about the store. Have we understood the impact of a billboard on the side of the road with no customized contact information on it? Are you not going to pay the phone bill because you're not sure what it's doing to benefit you?

The answers to all of the above are a resounding *no*. If you create a custom web page for your online product unique to those who clicked a link on Instagram and they only did that because they discovered your photo in a particular hashtag page while perusing the app...yeah, we can measure that.

The actual issue with fearing that there may not be enough to merit the cost and time associated with creating video content is that people are lazy. Yes. You might be lazy. If you went *allllll* the way to the point of getting on camera, creating video content that people like, uploading it, and letting the world know about it, but you didn't apply a measurable action to test all of it, then that's laziness.

You're not just doing this for attention. You're doing this for results. So why would you only go 75% of the way to make sure that it's succeeded?

Let's talk about your potential reach simply by uploading a video to the internet. On YouTube, there are more than one billion daily active users. *One billion.* Not to mention, the number of people watching daily is increasing 40% year over year. That is a massive amount of viewers, and you simply need to upload content for a chance to get in front of them.

Everyone's favorite social network, stalking website, and family scrapbook, Facebook, sees more than a billion daily active users as well. Facebook. YouTube. *Crushing* it when it comes to getting the average user's attention. Facebook is committed to video content for its users, so when you upload there, they give you extra-special treatment.

These days, you can create impactful video content simply by pressing a button on your phone, which is as low-production as it gets. Snapchat, the rabidly popular social network where all the kids went to hide from their parents who are on Facebook, sees more than 100 million daily active users. You just have to record ten-second video clips from your smartphone and you're sharing video online.

TV audiences are decreasing. People are texting and driving. Complainers send a tweet instead of calling customer service. Consumers aren't paying attention to the old marketing platforms that were hard to measure in the first place.

Oh, and let's keep something else in mind about sharing your message on social platforms. It's free. That's right. You just log in, and you're ready to go. The entry fee is $0.00.

Now is it going to be totally free? Absolutely not. There's going to be cost in the execution, of course. Nevertheless, to attend this amazingly huge cocktail party called social media and not have to pay for a ticket at the door is a massive advantage. The Super Bowl commercial space isn't free. Super Bowl 50 saw one of its largest viewing audiences in the event's history—111.4 million viewers. That's a fraction of the reach that social media has. Advertisers need to buy the slot and then spend many more millions of dollars on the production itself.

I'm asking you to consider publishing on a free social platform where people go to relate to each other which requires very little production and $0 barrier to entry. Sounds like a pretty good deal, right?

Whether this is apples to oranges or not, the bottom line is that it's about the bottom line. And if you want to measure it, you have to put in the work.

Properly planning out how this medium will be of value to you and determining what it will take to see those results is going to be the crucial step you must take to see return for success.

Yes. Your audience is online. Yes. You have the ability to speak directly to them. Yes. You can differentiate yourself from everyone else simply by leveraging video. You can make all of those decisions right now with no money up front (except maybe for that first video camera if you don't have a smartphone, and maybe you bought this book. Thank you.)

Stop making excuses just because not every step is going to be easy. ROI measurement included.

No More Fears

Okay, let's get real for a second.

The three fears we just discussed are big ones. They matter. You've likely considered all of them and maybe one rings truer than the others.

I know it's more than that. It's always more than that. We're talking about putting your face on camera for the entire world to see, and that's not even the scariest part. The scary thing is that if the entire world can see you, so can the people who matter to you most.

We may pretend we don't care about other people's opinions, but we do. Even those people who don't make us happy in any way but happen to be a factor in our thinking for some reason. We're constantly comparing our stuff with other people's, paying more attention to what someone else has rather than the things we have and could be grateful for.

We think about potential gossip. We know what people have said about others when they're not around, so why wouldn't they have a field day talking about us when we've left the room too?

What about those who are brutally honest? The ones who want to shock you with their hurtful words that aren't a reflection of you at all.

Judgment. Insecurity. Bullying. Negativity. Sadness.

If we could keep these things from hurting us, surely we would try. Yet, we're also imperfect humans who have probably leveraged these nasty tools when we were feeling vulnerable too.

Video is intense. Not only do you need the courage to do it, but you need to watch it back and learn from yourself. You need to share it with the world, even when it's not quite perfect. The only path to relatability is to be just that: a relatable, authentic person. Perfection is out of the question. Therefore, vulnerability is a necessity.

I can't stand on a pedestal and preach how much you need to embrace vulnerability. To be honest, I haven't embraced it at all.

I still want to be perfect. I still want to be better than everyone else. I still want to do the impossible. I don't want anyone else to know when I'm having a hard time accomplishing any of it. I want to be great at everything. It's a quality I've had my entire life.

I'm not great at everything. I'm really, really, really not. It makes me sad, but there are only good reasons as to why this is the case. I can't be great at everything if I'm truly focused on doing one thing the best.

I'm sure you'll be interested to hear that I'm absolutely terrible at writing this very book. I'm not good at this at all. It's the hardest thing I've ever done. Period. But I don't want anyone to know I'm struggling with it. (Well, I guess you'll know now.)

What I know for sure—and the reason I keep stroking these keys to get it done—is that my message is import-ant. It's too important to sit on and not share. I can't let this book stay inside me selfishly because I don't feel like writing and would rather break out a video camera. It has to happen because I know that so many people who support me and the work I've done so far want to see my work in a book they can learn from and share with others.

It's not going to be perfect. It's not going to be the best book on the shelves. But it will be my work. It will be a reflection of how much it means to me to share this information with you. That's my true purpose in all of this:

educating the people I want to help about something they want to understand.

If you're still hung up on how you couldn't possibly get on camera and make a video, please know how much I understand you right now. I really get you. I'm emotional even sharing this tiny bit of feeling with you here on these pages because it makes me uncomfortable. I'm fighting it because I know my small win in being vulnerable is one that will empower you to get past some of the fears you have about getting in front of a camera.

Don't let them stop you. People talk whether you're doing well or not. Jealousy and other people's sense of entitlement will never go away. Why scramble for someone else's acceptance when it's all up to you anyway?

Don't stop yourself. I promise to share my very best advice for you to do this in a way that will help you get past the hard beginnings. As long as you stay focused on the importance of your message and practice, we will do this together.

Let's get started.

PART TWO
VLOG LIKE A BOSS

CHAPTER FOUR
A SAVVY STRATEGY

In my career, there have been many perks for starting as a YouTuber rather than a business person.

The creative goggles always look a bit different when money is the motivator. That's why so many YouTube creators have gone on to make incredible amounts of money for uploading one video per week. They came into it for the love and not necessarily the paycheck.

You can recognize someone in this camp by asking them a simple question:

If all the money went away would you still create videos?

A true creator will answer yes. Don't get me wrong—there are plenty of people who started for the love of video and might choose a different path now. The community was there at the beginning and throughout. That makes the creator's mindset different and gives them a great advantage over everyone else who simply sees money in return for attention.

I've been one of those "for the love" kind of creators since 2009. It's never gone away. What made things all the more interesting was becoming a businesswoman with additional goals to reach. The landscape of why someone vlogs is a little bit different for businesspeople than for vloggers creating for the love of it.

Starting as a creator, I had the Schmittastic YouTube channel. This was a creative place for me to practice my video skills and build a community. It's where I got my start after the wedding video inspired me to dive into this passion. People were watching me hang out with my friends or take trips to Target and, incredibly, they were enjoying the experience. It was all fun and very personal.

When I started my business, the *why* for having a YouTube channel needed to be much more strategic. I had learned what it took to build a community for fun on the Schmittastic channel and wanted to leverage that talent for a new purpose moving forward. I needed an outlet where people could discover me for my work and potentially hire me, which required a content plan to teach people how they might use social media for business.

I couldn't just take the old YouTube channel and turn it into something else for a few reasons:

1. I planned to keep up the Schmittastic channel to showcase my personal side, as I had been doing, and didn't want to muddy those waters.
2. Even with just a few thousand subscribers, it didn't seem fair to flip the script on them when that's not why they subscribed in the first place.
3. I love, love, love the idea of starting fresh. Always. It's my favorite.

Thus the launch of Savvy Sexy Social, a new You-Tube channel for me to share ideas with those who may have a weakness in digital communication. A resource to subscribe to for actionable, helpful content that would also help me build my thought leadership in this new arena.

Your Why

Knowing your why is massively important. Not just in business or content creation, but in life. Without that reason to keep motivated through the slow, rough, mediocre and/or disappointing times, you're not going to see what success looks like. There are no shortcuts to the top. Just driven, focused people who finally get there someday.

Before you can get started with anything in the vlogging arena, you need to know why. Why is this important to you? Why is video content the answer? Why are you just a little bit better than everyone else? Why would people watch? Why would they subscribe?

Unwavering belief in my why is what's gotten me here today. I love vlogging, but I don't think love would have been enough to get me to the 650+ videos I have on my channel today. It was much more than that.

I vlog because I want to make people laugh.

I vlog because I want to help people be a better version of themselves.

I vlog because I want to drive business and build a career I love.

I vlog because it helps me be a better public speaker.

All of those things are what keep me going to create and push through. They are what make my goals worth reaching and waiting for.

As you're starting to think about your why, I want you to get honest with yourself. Don't fight the real reason you're here right now.

These days, with the internet displaying everyone else's "perfect" lives, it can be hard to remember what we truly want. We start to trick ourselves into thinking we know what we want because we measure ourselves against others who look like they have it very, very good.

Be super real with yourself. Stop fighting who you are. If you are doing this so you can live a completely location independent life and never have to report to a boss again, then perfect. If you're doing this because you need a platform to build your thought leadership and create a community of people who appreciate you because you don't feel appreciated in your own life, great. If you want to create videos because you think you're the most gorgeous person ever to walk the earth and that should be shared with the universe, by all means.

Do yourself a favor and don't lie about why you're doing this. You can save the pretty answer for the press release. (*LOL yeah right...by "press release," I mean Twitter.*) When you're pushing through your 20th video with a very slow-growing audience and barely any views or attention, you're going to want to remember why this matters to you.

Don't fake it. Get real. Be you and own it. That's the only way this video thing is going to work out for you. We only get one life. Stop messin' around with how you want it to be.

> When you're pushing through your 20th video with a very slow-growing audience and barely any views or attention, you're going to want to remember why this matters to you.

What is your why? Write it down.

Put it on a sticky note and look at it every day. You will find out quickly if your why is strong enough based on whether you continue to push through and execute.

Set Your Goals

Now that you have a good understanding of why this matters to you, let's talk about what starting to vlog looks like from a technical perspective.

Goals are important; this I'm sure you already know. They're even more important here because we don't want the obvious social proof to be the only thing at play in your mind.

Think subscribers. Followers. Likes. Sounds good, huh?

Adding up the number of people following you and using it as proof of success is what people in marketing call leveraging your "vanity metrics." Vanity metrics add an interesting curveball to measuring success online that sometimes distracts people from the goals they should really focus on. For example, if you're wondering how many YouTube subscribers to strive for and are comparing your channel to some of the most successful in the game, then you're focused on vanity metrics as your goal.

Look back at your why. Whether you wrote one or a few, do any of them reflect a desire to become the most subscribed YouTuber in history? No? Then you're putting too much weight in that vanity metric. That being said, it could still be a part of your goal measurement. It just shouldn't be the only thing. Arguably, even the person who wants to be the most subscribed YouTuber in history should have more to measure than just that number.

If you're vlogging because you have a business that you want to promote, then the number of followers you have can be a goal, but it will probably be #3 or #4 on your list. These numbers are important on some level. They help attract a targeted audience. Then again, if the content is just insanely helpful and your perfect viewer found it and decided to hire you, isn't that a big win too?

Maybe you don't care to be the biggest in the world, but you do want to get paid to do what you love. Take a travel vlogger, for instance. Getting free trips around the world and making money for it requires some level of influence. This is an example where vanity metrics play a stronger role in goal setting. But a travel vlogger's biggest goal is the number of offers they get from hotels and airlines to use their services in return for promotion.

The biggest thing to realize here is that goals will not be the same across the board. If you're reaching for someone else's goals, you're building someone else's dream. What good is that?

What does success look like to you? Visualize it. Feel what it feels like. Smile at what a win would be. Think of two to five things that would help you make this visualization a reality and make them specific. Numbers and metrics aren't a bad thing if they are for something that truly matters.

How much money will you make? How many sponsorships will you work for? How many video subscribers will you grow to? How many new clients will you bring in? How many press opportunities will request your presence? How much extra money per month will you make?

Write down the goals you have for this and keep them in a place you can look at, along with your why. There is probably one big one, right? One goal that makes you excited to get started. You're thinking that you can do it.

You can. You will. It just may not happen overnight, and you need to be willing to accept the journey of that process. Enjoy it, even. If you don't, this isn't the right place for you to be.

We're well on our way to setting up your strategy. The goal that's going to bring it all together should be in the front of your brain right now, but we need to discover a couple more items to get this thing on the right track.

We need to know who you're vlogging for.

The Audience

No matter why you started, no matter how big your goals are or what makes your wheels turn, no matter what you think—if no one watches your videos, none of that stuff matters.

This isn't insecurity talking. This isn't like "oh I'm so ugly, no one will watch" or "no one would ever watch my videos because they're not as good as everyone else's."

No. That's not what I'm talking about here nor am I ever going to allow that kind of negative self-talk. You can dismiss that immediately. Thank you very much.

Believe it or not, people want to support you. They're probably focused on themselves first, but they want other people to be a success in a way that benefits them. That's kind of a strange statement, I know, but my point is that we do want others to succeed—even if they're just getting started—because it means good things might happen for the rest of us. Including but not limited to you creating some awesome videos for us to watch.

Back to my original point: if no one is going to watch your videos, nothing else matters.

You might be reading this book because you're excited by the idea of creating video, and you think you could make some awesome videos to share with the world. You might be doing it for you before anyone else, but you can't make videos that only you would appreciate. That would defeat the purpose.

You have to envision what this content will do for someone else. What will it feel like? Will they laugh? Just a little or a lot? Will it make them take action in their lives in some way? What will they do next? What kind of person are they that they would be watching this video in the first place?

Knowing the ins and outs of your audience is a crucial part of being discovered by them. You must cross paths at some point, but the only way you're going to be able to do that is if you think about who they are right now—who they are without you in their life. Do they even know they need you yet? Obviously not. How in the world will they find out?

The key here is to meet your audience where they are at this moment so they can find out how much they love you.

To do that, you need to be clear about who they are and what they want. What do they do in their full-time job? Do they have a family? Are they a traveler? Do they have an affinity for coffee? (*Who doesn't?*)

Knowing your target demographic isn't just about age and gender anymore. Their interests, passions, online activities, and favorite hobbies are some of the most valuable characteristics you can know about a person.

Some of these characteristics you will already know because of the type of content you want to share, but then you can learn more as you start to make contact with your perfect viewer. Learn what life is really like for them. That's where content gets special. How can you make their everyday life a little better with video that is tailored to fit?

Make a list of characteristics and facts about your perfect viewer. How do they use the internet? What do they think about? What's their life like offline? What are the most important or pillar moments in their life?

When you write these ideas out, you are building what's called a viewer persona. I love the viewer persona exercise because as you think about these things, you will start to see a face and even come up with a name for this "person."

Naming your person is a great way to stay hyper-focused on who you're creating content for at all times. You won't stray into areas that would confuse your viewer, and you'll always present the environment that they feel natural in.

Meet the viewer persona for Savvy Sexy Social: Charlotte.

Charlotte is a millennial American socialite, both online and off. She's never satisfied with the status quo and is always determined to find happiness and fulfillment. She sees the opportunity in creating environments that will make an impact on the world and is starting to dabble in content creation because her ideas need to get out there. She thinks about how to become more successful in her life, take control, and become better at managing her weaknesses. She feels a sense of ownership for everything she does and takes steps to streamline work and get more organized and prepared for whatever comes her way. She enjoys working out (in theory, of course, but actually kind of hates it), attending events, watching Netflix series (sometimes bingeing on a low-key weekend), eating healthier (so she can sometimes eat naughtily), and playing with her dog. The most important moments of her life include achieving career milestones, spending time with family, and learning how to do something completely on her own.

Is everyone watching Savvy Sexy Social a Charlotte? Absolutely not. First of all, there are plenty of men watching, lots of non-millennials, both older and younger, and not everyone binge-watches Netflix or has a dog (sounds like a less than satisfactory life to me though, no offense).

But that is who the content of my YouTube channel is specifically created for. I'm more likely to pull that audience in and align with them as well as help many more people in this world who also enjoy the videos I share.

Just because you choose one person doesn't mean you don't help many. Don't be afraid to niche down. Give your viewer a name and think about them regularly. They're your new best friend. What would they be doing at this moment? How can that start a video idea?

When you get focused on the perfect viewer, the opportunities are endless, and before long, Charlotte will be calling you her favorite vlog.

Your Strategy Statement

Does all of this sound silly, determining your why, audience, and purpose for a vlog? Why bother with all this stuff if you're excited about creating awesome content and could just get started by hitting record?

Look, if I had started by asking and answering a bunch of questions, I probably wouldn't be here today. It's the action that matters. Your ideas don't until they become real to someone outside of your own head.

> It's the action that matters. Your ideas don't until they become real to someone outside of your own head.

You're reading this book, which means you're probably taking video seriously (or at least you trust me enough to think you should start to). With that in mind, I want you to be equipped with the best plan of attack possible. I gotchur back.

This is about the long run. This is a hard road, even if you love it and it's your deepest passion the way it is for me. When it becomes your everyday experience, it's a job, plain and simple. It can still burn you out. You can love it, but that doesn't mean you won't get burnt-out.

Burnout happens to everyone, but especially those who are executing fast and efficiently yet aren't seeing the results. You probably won't see what you want in your video brand for some time. Maybe you won't have to wait long at all, but it will never be soon enough. We may have goals, but even when we reach them, it's not always so obvious that it's time to celebrate.

For those times—the wins and the losses, the high points and the moments of questioning, the incredible feedback and the Negative Nancys—for every step of the process, you need your strategy to be as clear as possible.

You need to remember who, how, what, and why it matters so that you can recognize real wins and quickly move past low times.

You should memorize your strategy statement and keep it in mind every step of the way so you never waver on the plan. If you decide to pivot, you know where you started and how you're evolving. Your strategy statement will keep you confident in your purpose and moving forward, rather than backward, in your execution.

We already talked about all the elements you need to know in order to come up with your strategy statement. This is the easy part. You just need to fill in the blanks.

In as clear and simple terms as possible, answer the following questions:

1. Who are you vlogging for?

2. What do you vlog about?

3. Why are you creating a vlog at all?

The answers to each of these questions will help you create that strategy statement to keep your vlogging plan in focus.

Hopefully, you've written answers to these questions, and they're succinct. We're now going to combine those answers in a strategy statement. But before we do that, let me clarify something.

This statement is for you. It's not something you need to publish somewhere or share with the rest of the world. Pieces and parts might be worth including in a tagline or bio page, but this statement alone should simply keep your head straight on what you're doing. Focus is everything, and you're going to need a lot of it.

Don't be afraid to say why you're really doing this in answer to #3. I think we all like to come up with pretty answers like "to help save the planet" or "to impact millions of lives." Those are great reasons if they're real. Remember your *real* why.

With that in mind, please fill in your strategy statement below. Be specific. Be ruthless. Be clear.

"I help (answer to #1) by vlogging about (answer to #2) so that I can achieve (answer to #3)."

I help _____

by vlogging about _____

so that I can achieve _____.

Nice work. No matter what your next step is, that's a huge win right there, knowing the answers to why and how you're gonna vlog like a boss. Pat yourself on the back. It's time to make some videos.

CHAPTER FIVE
TOPNOTCH TALENT

The decisions you make about your vlog are going to set the tone for how you are received by any audience, not just your viewer persona. This business is all about how you make someone feel, how they talk about you to their friends, and how they repeat your incredible content back to someone who would also be a perfect viewer.

Knowing who your audience is and what you want to achieve is only the first step. Next, we need to decide what message you want people to repeat back. What will they say about you?

People may not remember every video they've watched or how they found you, but they will remember how you made them feel (if you made them feel anything). The goal is to have an impact and make a feeling occur, but you can only do that by being hyper-focused on who they are and how they operate. What makes your viewer's wheels turn or gets them excited?

The way to that kind of word-of-mouth with video is through talent. If you remember, we talked about this in the section about fear of personality. It's not about your personality. It's about your talent to reach people and share things that matter to them. This is *the* thing that causes someone to naturally talk about you—their true feelings. They want to advocate on your behalf.

You become a video expert when you focus on your why. Your why is going to come in handy for these steps because they can feel difficult. Some days it will seem easy, but most days not.

Here's what makes it all worth it: hearing someone tell their friend about you. Not because you told them to but because they couldn't help themselves. You made that happen.

They think you're magical because you share your life through video. You will know that you're magical because you did the hard work it took to have a community who will want to talk about you.

Whenever someone says, "Amy is a social media maven and YouTube rock star!" I get so excited. Not that I like to have my ego stroked (*okay, maybe I do*). It's because that's my brand. That's what the videos are about. The viewers understand and feel my brand.

Secretly, I know what they're really saying even if they don't. Between the lines, they're saying that my channel creates an emotional impact that makes them want to watch and talk about it. That's talent. Knowing the content is important, but leaving a feeling is talent.

So let's talk about how I achieved that and how you're going to do it as well.

Talent in video can be summed up in three letters. That's right. Just three: SRP.

Specialize.
Read.
Practice.

These are the three steps to video talent. If you only took away this one piece of advice from this entire book, you could still go on to vlogging success.

Let's unpack each of them.

Specialize

We talked about how hard it is to truly be an authentic version of yourself. The struggles people have with specializing, I believe, fall into the same category of fear. We want to be all things to all people. It's our nature, even if we don't like to say it out loud. If we had a choice, everyone would love us and find us helpful.

Unfortunately, you don't build a rabidly loyal audience when you are trying to please the entire world. Yet, people still try.

Being a generalist isn't a bad thing, but it's not a differentiator. It's just not. I want you to be different. I want people to remember your name. I don't want people to come to you to find out if there's someone that's perfect for this, I want them to come to you because they know *you're* perfect for this.

Specializing is a big step because it means going niche and not looking back. You need to set the expectation for your audience with what you offer and stay in that lane. You can have fun with it and weave in and around the lines, but there will never be a question about how your audience describes you to others.

Jeff Bezos of Amazon is credited with the quote, "A brand is what people say about you when you're not in the room." What do you want people to say about you without having to make it your elevator pitch? The only way to have any control over the feeling you instill in someone is to get hyper-focused.

> How are you great?
> How are you different?

If you think you're too niche, you're probably wrong.

Don't you want to be the *only*? Even if you're truly not and there is competition out there? Don't you want to be so talented and influential when you niche down and share your message that people will call you the "only one" in your field? They're not going to say you're the "only pet trainer." There's no way would that be correct. But you might be the "only trainer for people who have epileptic beagles with separation anxiety in their post-puppy years."

Man, could I have used someone like that. Beagle owner here. She's sleeping under the desk right now. Keyboard taps are her happy place which is why I'm her best friend. Yeah. That's why.

Get specialized in what you do because it's going to take competition completely out of the equation and give you an incredible space to own.

What did you say you would talk about in your strategy statement? Do you know of anyone else doing that? Are there are a lot of other people doing that? How are you special? How are you different?

You might already have an idea for how you can define this for yourself, or you might have to do some research. Ideally, it's both. But you must find it out if you want that infectious word-of-mouth treatment from your audience. Because no one is rushing around to tell their friends about "just another comedy channel" or "another Q&A show."

How are you great? How are you different? How can you make sure your audience knows it? That's what it means to specialize.

Read

As it pertains to video talent, reading means you need to read your audience. Knowing them backward and forward is a critical requirement of everything you do. If you're not making your content special for someone, you're simply creating videos to make yourself happy. I'm pretty sure that's not going to achieve the success you're looking for.

Reading your audience gives you information about them so you can know how your video might play a role in their day. This is the critical component to being discovered: share about what matters to your viewers.

What are their problems, thoughts, and queries? How can you show up there for them? You want to go where their eyeballs are. To do that, you need to know what they're thinking. What are they googling? What type of online activity do they enjoy? What are they doing when they're away from their devices? What keeps them up at night?

Reading is also going to help you with the specialization part of talent. Verifying that there is a need for what you do and why it matters is important for picking your focus and narrowing it. You need to read your audience and see the benefits to them before you decide to proclaim a message through video.

Everything you do is about who you help. Period. Nothing else matters.

When your perfect viewer finds you, give them an environment of content that makes them say, "This is exactly what I need." That moment—that connection between you and your viewer—is the beginning of what will be an incredible long-term relationship. They will be your brand advocate for as long as you decide to show up and cater to their struggles, needs, and desires.

If you want to create a video presence worth loving, my best piece of advice is to be just as much a viewer as you are a creator.

You must be in the shoes of your audience if you want to create the best experience for them. This applies to content design as well as content delivery. We're focusing on the design side for now, but keep it all in mind.

Your target demographic is already watching videos online. We've established that by going through the numbers of how video is being received online and how many different ranges of audiences are watching. Knowing that, it's time for you to see what they're seeing.

As a creator who is now being assigned the role of an avid viewer, dive into search and social and find out what vlog-type content you can subscribe to. It doesn't need to be similar to what you're hoping to talk about. You'll find you learn a lot by seeing what people who are outside of your scope are doing to speak to and engage their audience.

One of my biggest advantages as a creator-turned-business owner is that I had years of being an avid YouTube viewer and creator under my belt (and everything I'd created was for fun and not for the bottom line). However, you don't need to have started as a creator to get on the right foot.

You'll often find that the impact of videos has little to do with technology and editing knowledge as much as with the personality who is guiding the viewer through the content experience.

Watch. Take notes. What do you like? What don't you like? How do they make you feel? Do you want to do something similar or different?

It's not just about what you enjoy watching and potentially emulating in your own way. You also need to watch content that you see your audience engaging in. How do you find out if they're watching it? Search for what you think is relevant to your target and look at the comments. Really dig in. See their names and click to their profiles. Are they similar to who you've defined as your perfect viewer? Then you should be thinking about the fact that they took the time to comment on this video and that may mean they are a subscribed viewer and enjoying this channel. What is it that seems to resonate with them based on the comment and video?

This may sound like a lot of work. That's because it is. You can't know someone really, really well and create something perfect for them if you try to save time in the process. You just can't. But you can make time for this research if you want your videos to hit more than just your family and friends who will support you anyway.

Your viewers aren't just watching videos. You can learn a lot about them by seeing how they interact with each other on social media. What do they talk about when they send their 140-character press releases to the world? Where are they the most active? What trending topics seem to strike a chord?

Social and online media have made it the simplest way possible to learn more about anyone we want. That includes people who aren't famous and are simply enjoying the internet for the content and entertainment it provides them. It cannot be overstated that you must dissect what your perfect viewer is interested in. The more you know about them, the clearer your plan will become.

Specialize. Get niche. Stay niche. Read your viewer. Then vlog like a boss.

Because now you have to do it over and over again until it sticks.

Practice

This one is pretty self-explanatory. The only way to get better is to keep going. In video, that means pressing publish.

Sure! You can record a video, watch it, then drag that file to the trash and start over again.

Every time you opt for the trash and perfection, you miss out on an imperfect small win.

A small win is better than trash.

I can't wait to see people quoting that on Twitter.

I know it's tough watching yourself on video for the first time or maybe even the 100th time. It feels so personal. You watch. You close your eyes. You open them again. You're still there. You cringe. You puke a little in your mouth. It's a whole thing.

Without pressing publish, you didn't really practice. Recording something you intend to delete is not practice.

If I tried to make every video perfect before I clicked publish, I wouldn't be writing this book today. I'm proud to say that I have over 1,000 imperfect videos on the internet, because if they were indeed perfect, there might only be a couple of them online.

(I'm not as proud to say that approximately 85% of those imperfect videos are due to my hair being out of place. *Just giving an example....*)

Malcolm Gladwell said in his book *Outliers* that it takes 10,000 hours of practicing something to achieve mastery. 10,000 hours of video creation is a Long Way Away, even for me.

You'll never reach it unless you practice. And you need an audience to come along on that journey with you if you're going to get better on the way.

Publish. Publish. Publish. That's your job. Learn how to do this and get started as soon as you can. It doesn't matter if no one watches or if thousands watch. You must click "publish" if you're going to practice and become talented with video.

CHAPTER SIX
POLISHED PROGRAMMING

The hardest thing for any video creator is starting with a blank slate. It's easy for me to tell you to click publish, but you need a little something more to work with. Similar to writing, a blank sheet of paper could mean endless opportunities but also feels like the daunting start of nothingness.

Even as a seasoned vlogger, you do not want to have a blank slate all the time. It's exhausting. Thinking about what kind of video you're going to make next and starting from scratch every time is difficult for someone who needs to execute often and regularly. You need to set yourself up for success as much as possible, which is why you've started by doing so much research on your perfect viewer.

Knowing them well is likely spawning a lot of ideas in your mind of some videos you could create, or at least what kind of videos they'll be. We need to put some structure in this process so you always have an idea and that idea has its place.

There is a reason it was "easy" for me to post three videos a week for three years and then even more regularly after that. I was clear on the content I would share with my community—it had to fit my strategy statement.

Clarity means knowing what you do best and what you're passionate about. This should have come out in your final strategy statement in Chapter Four. With your strategy in mind and that passion guiding you, you can now determine the pillars of your content strategy that will help you with programming.

Bucketing

Programming in video means you're planning your content execution schedule. To do that, you need to get organized and focused. Start with a technique I call *bucketing*.

I'm a fairly organized person. I like to keep my house tidy. When it's time to clean out some drawers or move little things to a new place, I need a system. This is why I love buckets. Each container holds a specific kind of item, and even if some little knickknack hasn't found a home quite yet, it can sit in a bucket in the meantime.

As we start to work through your programming design and get a clearer idea of the actual videos you'll share, I want to use this house-cleaning analogy to break it down and make it practical. Every video has a category it belongs to, depending on its theme or topic. These categories are the "buckets" I want you to visualize as we start to design your content plan. Not only will they help you keep your sanity in the ever-constant content ideation process, but they will also represent specific areas you'll cover within the overarching promise of your channel.

By designing your theme buckets to fill with video topic ideas, you will keep your channel interesting yet predictable. Predictability is more enticing to a viewer than it sounds because it offers them a level of comfort that keeps them coming back as a loyal advocate.

Let me give an example. Let's say the strategy statement of your video presence is the following:

I help single working mothers by creating videos about how to make a delicious meal for their children in under 30 minutes so that I can increase awareness and sales of my cookbooks and potentially start a cookware line.

We're going to give this channel four buckets, perfect for an editorial calendar of one episode per week—one bucket for each week. (P.S. We're going to dive deeper into scheduling your editorial calendar in a bit, but let's just use this frequency for the sake of example.)

The buckets (video themes) might look like this:

Bucket #1: 10-Minute Breakfasts (first week of the month)
Bucket #2: Luxe Packed Lunches (second week of the month)
Bucket #3: 30-Minute Dinners (third week of the month)
Bucket #4: Delightful Desserts (last week of the month)

Each of these bucket themes is going to help the creator come up with new ideas rather than leave them looking at a blank slate every week. They give a very specific parameter of what qualifies as a potential video.

Next time a recipe comes to light that would be a perfect teaching moment, that idea has its bucket and therefore a place on the editorial calendar.

Found the perfect brownie recipe? Great. That goes in Bucket #4 and will be the last video of whatever month has an opening.

Let's try another example of buckets that allows you a little more flexibility. For the same channel, we're going to define them by format instead of theme.

They might look like this:

Bucket #1: Tutorial (first week of the month)
Bucket #2: Checklist (second week of the month)
Bucket #3: Review (third week of the month)
Bucket #4: Q&A (last week of the month)

The tutorial would obviously be how to make a meal in less than 30 minutes, but any meal could go in that bucket. The checklist could be an economical list of things to get at the grocery store or the top five items to keep in the kitchen no matter what. Reviewing could be anything from a tool to another publication's recipe. And of course, the all-important incorporation of engagement and inter-activity with a Q&A episode.

There's more flexibility in the buckets when you use format instead of theme, but you can see how they still help you put an idea in its proper place or get wheels turning if you need a video idea.

The latter example of bucketing is how I ran the You-Tube channel for Savvy Sexy Social for its first five years (only the buckets were for the days of the week since I uploaded Tuesday, Wednesday, and Thursday).

I played off the name of the channel to come up with those buckets:

Savvy Tuesday (savvy strategies for an online presence people will love)

Sexy Wednesday (how to make your content "sexy" for your audience—even if it's not super fun in the first place)

Social Thursday (social media platform tips and tricks to help you get further with your everyday online engagement)

Just because my buckets were publicly known doesn't mean yours need to be. As long as they are defined, and you stick with it, you will find success in bucketing. Simply having those buckets and using them to guide you will be predictable for your audience and incredibly helpful for you.

Decide how you want to bucket your content and keep it somewhere you look often until you have them memorized. I currently have six buckets, so I'm keeping the list in front of me on a sticky note pasted to my computer. When a video idea springs to mind, I can quickly look to make sure it has its proper place in my video brand design.

> Don't fail on account of not having enough ideas.

This step is far and away the reason Savvy Sexy Social content has been so consistent. For those creators who have become wildly successful—especially in a place like YouTube where getting started is a bit of a challenge—they followed some idea similar to the bucketing guide, and that's what kept their audience excited, guessing, subscribed, and yearning for more.

Don't fail on account of not having enough ideas. Set yourself up for success and inspire your ideas regularly by keeping in mind the themes that your perfect viewer has signed up for. You will quickly design a video brand that people will be able to explain and share with their friends.

Now it's time to answer everyone's favorite programming question: how often should you post a video?

How Often Should You Post?

"So, Amy. We've done a lot of planning, and I just want to get started. How often do I need to post a video?"

This is the biggest question I get asked about video content. It's a good, practical question, but it still points to a lot of things that could already be wrong with your approach.

All that aside for a minute, let me start with the answer you don't want: it totally depends.

It depends on you.

It depends on your audience.

It depends on the platform you choose.

It depends on the format.

There are a multitude of factors here, so there is no one clear path.

If you want the quick answer regarding the industry standards for YouTube uploads, it's once per week. That's what the reps from the YouTube NextUp program shared with us when I attended this past summer.

Let me talk about that for a minute, because a crazy interesting thing happened to me.

I had blocked off time when I would not be traveling so much so I could wake up and be focused every day on writing this book. It would be my main objective for the entire month of August.

Then, YouTube called. And when YouTube calls, you answer, especially if you're a YouTuber.

They let me know that I had been selected as a winner of their NextUp camp, which is a week-long program at one of their Spaces (this one was in New York City).

They invite winning applicants that have a good starting point on YouTube—between 10,000 and 100,000 subscribers—to come and be invested in by the video giant through teachings on YouTube success strategy, high video production, equipment education, and they receive a stipend for brand new equipment upgrades.

This was kinda crazy to me for a couple of reasons.

1. I never win anything, so WTF?!
2. This would come during the one period of time I'm not already traveling all over the place because I'm writing a book about how to vlog. Convenient.

Even though I was dedicated to getting this book done before the fall season speaking schedule picked up, there was no way I would pass up this opportunity and not leverage it as something more I could learn and therefore teach to you here in this book.

Probably the most discussed item among all the winners who participated in this program (there were 16 of us) was the consistency of uploading.

So you should feel pretty good about the fact that even YouTube channels with a following of 12,000, 50,000, 97,000, and everywhere in between were struggling with the concept of choosing a regular schedule.

We would go around the room and talk about how often we upload, and a lot of answers from creators went like, "Once per weeeeeek????" which sounds as confident as it looks on paper. They were shooting for once a week, but without a hard deadline, it was looking like every other week…maybe.

I was on the other end of the spectrum from a lot of the NextUp-ers. Most people didn't have a schedule. I've had a strict schedule since January 2013. I posted

Tuesday through Thursday for three years. Then, at the beginning of 2016, I decided to test the daily format: Monday through Friday, from January 1 until the end of March. Then April 2016 was the Savvy Sexy Social bi-annual event of "Vlog Every Day in April" or "VEDA" (the other time I do this is August). So April went to seven days a week.

After I had gone hardcore, posting daily on the channel for the first four months of the year, I went back to my three-days-a-week schedule but spread them out a bit more: Tuesday, Thursday, and Sunday. Spreading the videos apart helped me realize what was happening for all those years of back-to-back videos, Tuesday through Thursday.

When you upload something to YouTube, it has about 48 hours to prove whether or not it's going to fly in the long-term. It's all based on what your viewers do to engage with it right away.

Now, of course, a video can take off or go viral long after it's been posted. But you can usually tell in the first 48 hours (and I've also seen deeper research on this from much larger channels with a great deal more data to measure) whether or not a video is going to be a success, failure, or just the usual.

When you're uploading again in that period of 48 hours, you're disrupting the interaction your subscribers may have with that previous new release. Because now there is a new one in the way of the other one in the subscription feed, as well as your promotional channels. Too much going on.

Sure, they could watch both. Sure, if they love you, they will watch all of them. However, we have to remember how little time people have. Even if they're not busy people, they're distracted. You might lose them.

So I spaced out the uploads to at least 48 hours apart and started to see a little more success, but nothing too crazy.

It didn't occur to me until we were having this discussion in New York: three times a week is a lot for YouTube. "The industry standard is once per week, and as creators start to grow their success, they will start to test a second episode on their main channel," my YouTube liaison shared with me during our one-on-one conference.

Man. I'm so glad I was writing this book and took a break from it to go to this camp. I feel like I wouldn't have been able to tell you this without the chops to back it up because my experience had been different. And now, since I've been back, everything is starting to change because of altering the posting schedule.

It was very difficult for me to go down to one video per week, even on the advice of YouTube. I knew I needed to pare down a little, but for years I've been a trusted resource for my audience, regularly uploading three to five times per week, and one video seemed like a stretch.

I will say, there's the industry standard and then there's the relationship you've built with your audience. It's important to take both into account, but also give credit to each. One might be more flexible than the other. Maybe the more flexible one is your audience. There's only one way to find out.

Ask.

If you're ever as unsure as I was at this moment, here is my advice: poll your audience.

Don't have an audience? That's okay. Poll people who you know will lift you higher and support you, and ask them what they think.

I ran a poll on Twitter *immediately* after the chat with my YouTube liaison to see what my trusted community had to say. Here are the results:

Amy #VlogBoss ✓
@Schmittastic

How many videos per week do you watch from
my YouTube channel? (Tell the truth!)

39% 0

34% 1 or 2

20% Every new upload! (3/wk)

7% MORE! binge and repeat...

133 votes · Final results

RETWEETS   LIKES
2   12

1:44 PM - 10 Aug 2016 from Manhattan, NY

↩ 7   ⟲ 2   ♥ 12   ⊪   ···

Obviously, it is a little disheartening to see that some
people don't watch my videos. But hey, these are my
Twitter followers, not my YouTube subscribers. I wanted
to include that option to be fair. Also, there were more
votes if you want to count the people who don't like to
follow the rules. Those people left me tweet replies and
were mostly enthusiastic viewers who probably watched
every single new episode.

When 73% of voters say they watch between zero
and two of my videos on a weekly basis and I'm uploading
three or more, that's a clear indication that something isn't
right. I am really good at slamming out a video, but what
if I just put a little more effort into fewer videos? Would
more of those "zeros" watch?

The following weekend, I posted a recap vlog about
how the NextUp camp went, which was a fairly long video
for me. At the end, I had a heart-to-heart with my viewers and asked them to help me make this determination
since the poll on Twitter was starting to convince me to

make a change. I had to be sure my subscribers had the same mindset.

I knew that the audience I had retained until the end of this video—with the content being much longer than usual—would be the most valuable people to poll:

Here are the results:

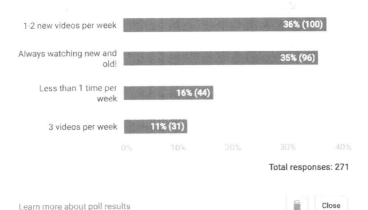

That poll you see in the YouTube video is a function of YouTube Cards, an incredible feature you should use, and we will talk more about that later. Look at those results!

271 people replied (which is 9% of the total view count for the video.) The winning result was the option of one to two videos per week. Now, the "always watching new and old!" I included for the enthusiastic superfans, and that is not a vote to discount. They very well could be watching every video and rewatching old. The number of people who said they watch three videos per week was very low, and that's the number of times I was publishing at that point. That's the reason for concern.

Those same people who say they're always watching new and old are going to appreciate an increase in quality with fewer videos because they don't mind going back and watching archives when they need a little more. This makes for a richer experience for new fans and superfans alike.

In the short time since I've been back from the NextUp program, I've been uploading two days a week. I chose Tuesdays because Savvy Tuesday has been around since the beginning and has always been a good day for me to make time to upload. I like Sundays because I feel like you can touch more people who have a hard time watching during the week. By posting Sundays and Tuesdays, they're spaced out enough to breathe, and there's plenty of time the rest of the week for both videos to perform at their best.

I've already seen a crazy difference in reception. Granted, I'm approaching content differently now that I have more time to spend on quality, but average views are up 150% on a normal upload simply by decreasing frequency.

I went into YouTube with stability and structure in my content schedule while everyone else is having a hard time just choosing a day that they will upload religiously. But both sides need to look at things a little differently to get those sweet spot results.

Like I said, it's going to depend on your format. This is what it's like with YouTube: they want you to post once a week, and they have a lot of data to prove that's the best consistency.

I hope the fact that I'm going through this transition right now is helpful for you to hear, even as it's happening. More than anything, I want you to feel confident in your chosen schedule. I know you're probably thinking how hard it's going to be to post once per week, but you should also feel excited about that schedule because it's the optimal decision to make.

That being said, uploading more frequently at the beginning is likely a good plan as well. Especially when you're publishing to a community of zero subscribers. The reason for this is an investment in your archives.

Let's say you upload a video, and it's doing well with social shares. People are watching and commenting. They heard about you from their friend on Facebook. After they finish the video, they click over to your YouTube channel to see what else you have to offer and—*gasp*—there's nothing else there.

Unfortunately, a sleepy YouTube channel makes it hard to encourage subscribers. You need to set a channel up for success if you want to attract staying customers. That's why uploading a little more often, or even launching with three or five episodes instead of one, would be a good decision.

All of this makes sense for the average channel, but what if you report the news? Maybe it should be a daily channel. Maybe your videos are only one minute long, so you were hoping for a three-days-a-week schedule.

Like I said, it depends.

You need to think about your format and the feasibility of creating something worth sharing. How often should it be done and how often can you do it? Start from a manageable place so that you can grow in frequency rather than burning yourself out when no one is watching. I promise you: it will be worth it to think long-term.

When you look at your buckets, think about the logistics so you can fully wrap your mind around the time it will take and how to get the most mileage out of that content. You don't need to know your exact schedule right now, but as you think through topic ideas (in the next section), you'll start to grasp the time and effort that's going to go into this.

Programming Design

We've worked out the buckets that will guide you through the content structure process. We've also had the crazy interesting and extensive conversation about choosing your frequency.

These two worlds now need to collide. The buckets are going to help you plan individual topics (which will be what we discuss next), but first, they need to have at least a loose connection to your schedule so you can get an idea of what execution from a time management perspective looks like.

For instance: in the example of the Cooking Channel we talked about four buckets, and for the sake of ease we decided on one video per week. That's one video for each bucket throughout one month of content.

Sun	Mon	Tues	Wed	Thurs	Fri	Sat
			10-Min Breakfast			
			Luxe-Packed Lunch			
			30-Min Dinners			
			Delightful Desserts			

You could instead go the route I did in Savvy Sexy Social's early years and publish three buckets three times per week:

Sun	Mon	Tues	Wed	Thurs	Fri	Sat
		Savvy Tuesday	Sexy Wednesday	Social Thursday		
		Savvy Tuesday	Sexy Wednesday	Social Thursday		
		Savvy Tuesday	Sexy Wednesday	Social Thursday		
		Savvy Tuesday	Sexy Wednesday	Social Thursday		

As you're building from the buckets and thinking about your schedule, diagraming this structure and keeping it in mind is going to be a massive help as we go into editorial planning. Without even knowing what your individual video ideas are yet, you have an entire month of content planned and you need to start allocating time to film and create.

This, my friend, is quite the opposite of a blank slate. It's a hand-holding calendar and the best friend you could have to stay consistent with your content creation.

Take the time to map out what this will look like for you. Only posting a couple of times a month? It doesn't matter. Look at it. Look at the dates. Think about the next month and see where the time needs to be scheduled to get these videos done.

Once you've reserved the time on the calendar, all that's left is to fill in those topics with specific video subject matter and get them done! Let's discuss how you can keep this organization readily available for when those great ideas pop up and make it even easier for you to get the job done.

Topic Brainstorm

It's finally time to talk about what you're going to talk about. Exciting, huh?

Now that you know your strategy, audience, and the buckets you want to fill, it should be easy, right? Not exactly. If it were easy, neither of us would be here.

Let's go back to your audience and talk about what's on their mind. If you're going to create videos they cannot resist, it needs to strike a chord with them. What do they think about? What are their problems?

Knowing their pain points and struggles, what they enjoy for entertainment, and how they like to learn are critical to developing content that will immediately grip your perfect viewer.

Make a list of what keeps your audience curious. What questions are they asking? Better yet, what are they googling? See if you can write down ten questions you have heard your perfect viewer ask you, either directly or indirectly in some way.

Having a starting point of just ten questions that get into the mindset of your audience will help you come up with many ideas for content. Everything needs to come back to helping people, and when you know exactly what they want help with, you can dive into a specific idea related to it.

I like to look at trends when I'm thinking about my audience. Researching popular search terms on YouTube and Google might give you an idea of some relevant questions people have and help you better understand your audience.

A great option for this is YouTube predictive search. That's the recommendation of search queries that drops down as you're typing into the search bar (seen below). By putting in some generic starter terms, you can see the most popular searches on YouTube for that phrase. Here are tons of ideas to consider that you know have traction with a widespread audience.

Also keep in mind that your viewer may have a question and not even know it. Go beyond the surface questions they ask and think more deeply about where those inquiries are coming from. You're their expert, so considering how you can help is important. Making it relevant is key.

If you have a list of ten questions or inquiries in front of you, think about the different ways and types of videos that could answer those questions.

I want to give you a list of video templates that have been proven successful and which will give you a good start to coming up with lots of video ideas from one single question.

Keeping one of your written questions in mind right now, use the following list to start getting your wheels turning on the different ways you can create videos to answer that question:

- Industry News
- Tutorial/How-to
- DIY (Do it Yourself)
- Reaction
- Top Five List (what I like to call a listicle)
- Ultimate Guide
- Case Study
- Recap/Roundup
- Tips and Tricks
- Myths and Misconceptions
- People Connection (Introduce someone new on your channel.)
- The Right Way or The Wrong Way
- Crowdsourced
- Books
- Reviews
- Controversial/Rant
- Problem/Solution
- FAQ
- Prediction
- Research
- Checklist
- Definition
- Series
- Interview
- Timely
- Tools
- Resources
- Inspirational
- Behind-the-Scenes
- Curated

Let's use our earlier example of the Cooking Channel for busy single moms. Let's say a busy single mom is asking the question, "How do I make sure my kids are eating healthy foods when we're always on the run?"

Using our list of templates here, we can come up with lots of ways to answer her questions:

- Tips and Tricks—*Veggies and Packed Lunch: The Trick to Make Sure They Eat It*
- Checklist—*The Busy Mom Healthy Grocery List*
- Listicle—*5 Yummy Veggie Snacks Your Kids Will Love*
- Research—*Eat Your Veggies! Why Your Approach is All Wrong*
- Review—*Banana Chips: Do the Kids Approve?*

I took one question and, using templates, came up with five different video topics on the fly that could potentially answer that question. This is a good time to make the point that it may seem like you're talking about the same thing all the time, and that's okay. You're an expert. A thought leader. An authority. You're supposed to know one or two things really, really well. This is a great example of how that can be the case, but the content can continue to flow, and you can keep things interesting.

You'll want to create this list and also do some research on each topic you think you want to proceed with to see if there are other results or competition in the space. Meaning, check out search results for the topic and see what comes up. If there are lots of results that are similar, this can be good or bad. It's good because you know there is demand. It's bad because you have to stand out to rise in the rankings.

By taking ten questions and breaking them down into different topics, using templates to answer them three different ways, you are well on your way to a full editorial calendar of 30 topics. That's a video idea for every day of the month! (Not that that's your schedule, but you get the point.)

Pulling it Together

Having a full programming calendar is all about setting yourself up for success. You know your strategy. You have your buckets for different types of content. You're wrapping your mind around how often you want to publish. You've brainstormed some video ideas.

It's critical to create a system that will help you keep this going. It doesn't have to be fancy or complicated. It doesn't even need a certain kind of editorial calendar software to track it all. It just needs to work for you.

Personally, I have a couple of logistics at play to keep my editorial plan full. First, I keep a sticky note of my buckets on the computer in front of me. It's the first thing I look at when I come up with a video idea so I make sure it has a special place in my content strategy.

Next, I use Evernote to keep track of ideas. You can use any note-taking app (or even pen and paper, if you like) for this.

I keep a list of ideas in one note. I create a table (as seen below) so I can lay everything out in its proper place. The columns list the buckets, and whenever I have an idea, I add it to the column that corresponds to the correct bucket and create lists that way. It's so much easier than just having a long list of ideas, especially when there may be one area that you want to do more vlogging in but you lack ideas. It may spur you to focus on brainstorming for that list in particular when you can set aside time.

When you have ideas on the fly, it's so important to give them a place. All your video topics need to be stored somewhere so you can easily identify all your ideas and plan them on the calendar. If you have some ideas in a note on your phone and other ideas on a sticky note and a few more on the whiteboard of your refrigerator, your organization is going to go awry. Even if you have ideas, it will feel like you have none.

If you organize nothing else, organize this. If you would prefer to do your videos at the last minute and on the fly, at least the one thing you have going for you is the list of ideas to pull from when you sit down to film.

Here's an example of the table I talked about with our previous example of the Cooking Channel:

10-Min Breakfasts	Luxe-Packed Lunch	30-Min Dinners	Delightful Desserts
The Kids Review! Banana Chips	Veggies and Packed Lunch: The Trick to Make Sure They Eat It	The Busy Mom Healthy Grocery List	
	5 Yummy Veggie Snacks They'll Love	Eat Your Veggies! Why Your Approach is All Wrong	

As you can see here, from the buckets we designed and the topics we came up with, each idea has its place in the structure of the programming. We can also see that we need to come up with more breakfast ideas and the dessert options are entirely lacking. If it's been a while for desserts on the channel, maybe we need to sit down and brainstorm a few so we can get this column filling up again.

But regardless, every time a new idea comes in, it has its place. It's easy to make sure you have equal amounts of each type of video planned on the calendar, and you won't feel like you're pulling ideas from who-knows-where to make sure you get the video out ASAP.

My take on video will always be that you just need to get started. If you have one idea right now, then run with it. But when you hear the advice to "just get started," that doesn't mean to "just keep winging it" too. Getting started is the hardest part, but keeping it up without a programming plan to guide you throughout the execution process is even harder.

Again, it's about setting yourself up for success. Take the time to develop this list, and you will be thanking yourself for being on top of things as you become better at managing your time. Before you know it, you'll have close to 700 videos like me. I stuck with the plan and got the videos done on time, every time.

You don't need a viral video to be a success. You need to prove you can show up. This is the path to making that happen and vlogging like a boss.

Your wheels are turning now. You might even have a list full of ideas to go along with your new strategy and ambition. In the next chapter, it's all about learning the formula for a video that will keep your viewer hooked.

CHAPTER SEVEN
A FABULOUS FORMULA

Let's just get past something really important right now.

Your first video always sucks.

If you've made a video already and are using this book to improve, then you know this. But if you haven't set foot in front of the lens of a camera because you're afraid of how it will turn out, you're right to feel that way.

I'm not going to sugarcoat because that wouldn't be fair to you.

The reality is that you are standing in front of an inanimate object and trying to talk to it like it's a human being. That's weird. It's an obstacle we have to do deal with, especially that first go around.

It's safe to say your first video is going to suck. My first video sucked. Some of the most popular video creators in the world have some pretty wretched work from their beginnings. It's okay to suck at first.

The key is letting yourself have a beginning and pushing through it. And the more you arm yourself with the information that helps you make the video as good as it can be at that moment, the better you'll be no matter what the state of your video personality.

In the spring of 2015, I hosted my first-ever video workshop series called Savvy Sexy Social LIVE. It came to several cities, and people could attend for a day to learn the process of developing video programming to grow brand awareness. I wanted to teach a curriculum that would be easy for the attendees to understand and help them create the best video every time—not just that day but also when they left and started executing on the new strategies they learned.

This led to the design of my Authority Video Formula, which we're going to dive into in this chapter. The goal of this formula is to play the role of your guide when you get in front of the camera—fully anticipating to suck but hoping to stay on track— so that you can create a helpful, valuable video that is good enough to publish and help you start to build your video archives.

If you're going to have to suffer through sucking on camera, let's at least try not to let the audience know you're feeling that way. Power through the content as effectively as possible.

Please see the pictured formula and follow along with the description of each step. The visual nature of the formula is the winning feature here because you can easily draw it for yourself, print it out, or keep the image saved on your desktop or phone so it can be there as a quick reminder at a glance when it's time to create.

Before I walk you through each step of the formula, I do want to give a disclaimer of sorts. The formula was originally created and has continued to be tweaked for a YouTube video environment. The world of video is changing daily with new platforms supporting native video. (When I say *native*, I mean when you upload a video directly to the social platform you want to share it on, rather than posting a link to another destination.) You obviously wouldn't be able to follow this formula in a ten-second video Snap on Snapchat, unless you're a miracle worker.

There's also live video streaming—a very different scenario where diving into the content quickly is important. It's not usually the best tactic to do this at the beginning because you want to welcome people into the stream session to have a little bit of an audience before you start going too deep into details.

So just keep in mind that wherever you're going to upload, there is a context to that platform. The formula may guide you through the bulk of delivering the content, but you'll also need to take into consideration anything that's special about where you want to share your work. Treating each social network differently (because they are different) is a great way to get ahead of most people in a loud social media world. More on that later.

Let's walk through my Authority Video Formula.

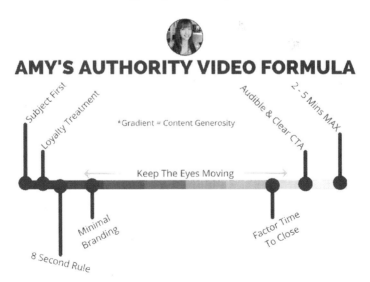

AMY'S AUTHORITY VIDEO FORMULA

Subject First

Loyalty Treatment

*Gradient = Content Generosity

Audible & Clear CTA

2 - 5 Mins MAX

Keep The Eyes Moving

Minimal Branding

Factor Time To Close

8 Second Rule

Subject First

The first moments of your video are the most critical. It doesn't matter how creative your content is or the awesome plans you have for your video. If you don't make it abundantly clear from the beginning that your viewers have made the right choice by clicking play, you will lose them. The rest of the video won't matter at all.

As video creators, we want to have more minutes watched. More time on-screen with our potential customers and audience members. The fate of your video is often decided by the very first image seen.

The main subject of your video needs to be in the frame the first moment viewers are watching. In most cases, you'll be like me, and the subject of the video is a person who will be taking the audience through the video content. The on-camera personality serves as the tour guide of this journey, and so their face is critical from the very beginning.

There's also an incredible upside to the main subject of the video being a person. The face of another human being is quite relatable for a viewer, who also has a face. That reliability goes a very long way, as obvious and silly as it may sound. As people, we crave human connection, and that's the entire upside of video—you're able to recreate that connection in a human and personal way. When your subject is a person, don't waste any time getting their face on the screen. Their welcome, no matter how it's done or said, is critical to give the viewer confidence about spending their time watching the rest of this video.

Like I said, for the most part, this will be the case. There will be a human in the video, therefore, they are the subject. Even what if the video is about, let's say, a product that's being reviewed? The role of a human is very important, but I also recommend that you introduce the product into the frame at the beginning of the video. Ideally, you would have both the person and the product, but as long as both happen in the first few seconds of the video, they don't necessarily need to be in the same frame.

The entire goal with "subject first" is that we instill confidence in our audience that we're going to offer them the best possible video. A human connection is huge and practically required these days. It should be presented immediately. If you're talking about how to use a device or reviewing a particular product, prove that you have that item. Bringing it into the very beginning of the video so that the audience has something to look at immediately helps as well. Showing that you're not just talking about something you've never touched or can show off will put you ahead of the competition.

Let's talk about an example of subject first that's more of a circumstance than a human or a product. There is massive demand in the beauty space for tutorials on how to do things with different types of makeup or recreating a hairstyle. The subject, in this case, is still going to be a human, but it's also going to be the result of the video. The most successful video creators are showing the beautiful results at the beginning of the video so that viewers will *then* decide to watch the tutorial. It may seem backward and that you would want to save the big reveal for the end, but in the world of tutorial videos, that's the worst thing you could do.

Subject first means that you reveal the best part at the beginning. It's all about retaining that viewer, and if they see something from the start that gets them excited, you have a good chance of keeping them for at least half the video. Which is considered pretty good these days.

Don't waste time impressing your viewers with your talent, product, or result. Subject first!

Loyalty Treatment

This is my favorite tip from the formula because a) it's extremely effective, b) it's a little controversial, and c) it differentiates the powerful creators from the amateurs.

"Loyalty Treatment" is the mentality of bringing every viewer into your video as if they have been watching every single episode you've ever created. You can do this even if you're creating your first video.

Picture this. You're kicking off the most incredible party train. It's going to be full of great times, awesome people, and you. Every time it makes a stop, people can get on, but you don't have to start over. They're just getting on board wherever it made sense for their journey. So you just keep rockin' what you're doing

> Discovering your content has nothing to do with you and everything to do with where they are in their life, their state of mind right now, and their need to watch your video.

and they will catch up. They probably got on board that day because of something they saw happening on your party train that was interesting or a little different from someone else's. Maybe they saw something they've been craving to see for a long time, so they jumped on to learn more. Your job is just to keep the train running!

When the new people get on, are you going to stop the music to explain what the new people should know first before they can feel included in the group? Nah! Why would you stop the party for some boring logistics when everyone is already having a great time, even the new people? Keep the train running.

What does this mean in real life when it's time to create that video? Simple. Don't put the video on hold for your introduction, bio, or elevator pitch.

When you start a video with your long-winded expla-
nation of who you are and why you're making the video
because of what you do and what you're hoping people
will want to do later, you're essentially giving an unwel-
come call to action (also known as a "CTA," something
you'll hear quite a bit more about in this book—remember
that term). They just got here! It's the first few seconds
of the video, and your viewer wants to know if this was
the right decision based on the party train they wanted
to get on to learn something new or be entertained, and
you're stopping the process to tell them things they don't
care about. More importantly, you haven't earned it yet.

Your elevator pitch is a pitch, which also means it's
a CTA. It's not the right way to start a video, nor is it the
right way to start a relationship with someone who is
meeting you for any reason other than they heard you
were cool. They saw the link to your video in a social
feed. Your result showed up in a search. Discovering your
content has nothing to do with you and everything to do
with where they are in their life, their state of mind right
now, and their need to watch your video.

Don't interrupt that.

If you're lucky enough to get this viewer in the first
place, the last thing you want to tell them is how they can
learn more about you on your website.

There's no need to worry! You're going to get your
chance. It's just not going to help you to lead off with it.
You have to give, give, and then give some more before
someone becomes interested in giving you anything in
return. That comes later in the formula.

I'm essentially telling you that when you start filming
your video, begin with your subject. Dive straight into the
content with zero introduction of yourself. Zero. I'm sure
that sounds crazy right now because you would think at
the very least you should share your name. I'm not saying

you can't, but every moment at the beginning is extremely precious. If who you are and what you do is not the reason someone clicked on the video in the first place, it doesn't make sense to waste time with the extra fluff.

8-Second Rule

We've talked about making sure you put the subject first in every video and how you need to treat your audience as if they are loyal so they will become just that. The reason for those two very critical pieces of advice is the 8-Second Rule.

The 8-Second Rule is a simple one, and if I'm quite honest, it may not be completely accurate anymore. Still, we will use it as a very important reminder.

Eight seconds is the time it takes a viewer on You- Tube to decide between watching the rest of your video and bailing. Whatever you've chosen to do in those first moments will either keep someone for many more minutes or send them packing immediately.

Remember, this rule applies specifically to YouTube because YouTube is a place where people watch video with intention. Someone finds the video and clicks play, in which case the audio and the video come on together. This is not true for Facebook. A video uploaded natively that shows up on the News Feed will autoplay whether a viewer is truly interested in it or not, and the audio will be muted. It's a very different decision-making process. If you don't want to watch it, you just keep scrolling. If you do, you click on it, and it will continue to play but with the audio on.

Ah, Facebook video. So seamless and yet so crappy for a video creator.

But back to the 8-Second Rule. For intentional video, like on YouTube, this marker is critical. You're already in good shape if you followed the first tips in the formula, but you're also under timing pressure to get into the content quickly. By that 8-second mark, if you haven't started talking about the relevance of the video and why someone has arrived there in the first place, you still have a chance of losing them.

Regardless of whether the metric is eight seconds today or three seconds a year from now, the lesson here is to dive into the content quickly. Do not waste time being generous with your advice, tutorial, entertainment, etc. This is all part of the process to show your audience you mean business about delivering on your promise.

By the way, as a beginning creator, I would think you're feeling pretty confident about the next time you kick off a video. I'm giving you permission and the exact process to make this experience as pain-free and simple as possible. By focusing on what you know and the message that your audience needs to receive, you're going to have no problem diving right in and feeling confident about what you're doing. No time to screw around with theme songs, awkward introductions, and the lead up to why everyone has gathered here today.

Just get to it!

Minimal Branding

"Whatever happened to predictability? The milkman, the paperboy, evening TV?"

If you know those lyrics, we can be friends.

As a kid, I used to watch Full House every week with my family, along with every other 30-minute sitcom on TV that made up the TGIF lineup. It was so much fun to tune into my favorite characters, but even more so to sing the theme song that set the tone for the episode.

The same theme song. The same video montage. The same logo. Quite literally *predictability*.

That was the 90s. It was a faster time compared to where we had been, but a much slower time than today.

Have you noticed that when you watch television now, the opening theme songs and videos are significantly shorter? If they exist at all. We even see the credits scrolling over the content of the episode for a good 20 minutes into a 1-hour show because they can't be fit into the now very short opening theme.

Except for House of Cards. *I love that show, but why is their theme song so freakin' long?*

Times have changed. We are a fast-moving society and we don't have time for these video sequences that are holding us back from getting to the good content. The new episode. The exciting drama. Just gimme the good stuff!

Well, if they're not even doing this on television anymore, why would you have a long title sequence for your online video? It's even less appropriate in this situation because your viewer probably found you in search or a social feed and may or may not be that loyal of a viewer yet. Are you really going to waste time with fancy branding instead of getting to the content you promised?

Look, I know how excited you were to send your branding to an outside company and have them write you a jingle, film you having the time of your life, and stamp your logo on it so you could use this 15 seconds of happiness in every episode. But as I've said, good video is video you make for someone else. Someone specific. This title sequence would be just for you. Last I checked, I don't think you were coming to me for advice on how to get you to like your own content.

However, I do think the integration of branding can be effective if done well at the beginning of the video. As long as you stick to the formula, it will be a great complement rather than a massive detractor.

If you like the idea of cutting away to a scene of your branding, you just need to make it significantly shorter. No more than two or three seconds. Enough time for your logo to be on-screen. Maybe some other text information like the episode title. A bit of music to fade it in and out seamlessly.

That's a simple idea, but not my favorite. The best branding I see early in a video is when it is integrated into the content of that episode. It doesn't mean it has to be different every time, but it's a nicer experience because it doesn't feel like you're taking someone out of one scenario and into another. The branding shows up in the viewer's current experience, and it's a nice reminder instead.

This essentially means editing your video together and leaving it as it is. However, you can overlay your branding onto the content at strategic moments. This is so that you don't have to take away from the content to show yourself off.

Now, I frequently get this feedback about this part of the formula, as well as others, "But there are plenty of content creators and video makers who are not following this advice and are uber-successful."

Yes. That's true. I'm not saying that my advice is the only way to success because I have a lot of ways I can grow. However, I'm also a big opponent of comparing yourself to others. Especially when you're starting from scratch and the person you're watching has been successful and took a lot of time and effort and work to get to where they are over many years.

Things are just not the same when no one knows who you are. Period.

If you want to play a 15-second branding sequence before you give the viewer the time of day about why they showed up to watch in the first place, be my guest. My job is to tell you what I think is going to turn casual discovery viewers into rabidly loyal subscribers. In my opinion, wasting their time with what makes you happy is not going to do that.

I know you're awesome. You know you're awesome. But they don't know yet. So can we please prove it first?

If you still think it would be awesome to have a 15-second montage of how awesome you are, create it for placement in a YouTube channel trailer or on your About page. Don't add it to every video and make your timestamp (length of video) longer than it already needs to be.

Content Generosity

The reason content marketing works so well is that people want to be in-the-know and they are constantly searching for new information. They're looking and looking, searching and scrolling, waiting for you to step up and tell them what they want to know.

Then they find it. Your video. They click play. You're bringing them in so easily and clearly and keeping good time. You haven't gone to town with a brand sequence, and you don't seem to mind that they aren't sure who you are yet. You just want to dive in.

And you deliver. You are generous with your content and give that viewer exactly what they hoped they'd signed up for. By the end, they are dying to know who you are and what you do and what you want them to do next.

Content generosity is very important because this is the "thing" that they wanted. Now you need to keep them tuned in long enough to get your CTA!

What you do during this time is going to make someone feel they got their time's worth by choosing this video instead of running for the hills at the first sign of unworthiness.

Content generosity doesn't mean you have the right to stand in front of a camera and go all college professor on me. Just because you know a lot on the headlined topic of this video doesn't mean you need to tell the viewers everything. This is where most people get into trouble and say, "Amy, there was no way I could give my opinion on this topic and have the video be less than seven minutes." Actually, there is a way. You didn't try.

Let me digress here. Focus is everything. Focus is the biggest thing. If your video seems all over the place, even if everything has to do with the subject, you will lose the attention of your viewer. They can only handle so much, and the value you bring is so great. The focus you design for your content is important because it will keep you on track for a video that makes sense and makes someone want more.

Now, that being the case, that's not what I meant about content generosity. I want you to have focus so that your video is the best possible product every time, but you must also get rid of the fear of sharing what you know.

I'm often asked if a client should hold something close to the vest so the competitors won't steal it or withhold information because it's how they make a buck.

Most of the time the answer is no. You shouldn't hold anything back because it's information that they might get elsewhere if they don't get it from you. Then you lost the opportunity to be their thought leader and inside track. Why keep it to yourself if others aren't?

The rule of thumb in this is that you obviously don't want to release intellectual property that is yours and would be detrimental to business if you share it. Clearly, we're not going to get the actual recipe for Coca-Cola because that's their intellectual property. However, if a soufflé chef won't show you how to make one because they would rather you hire them to make it, they're missing the point entirely.

Be generous with what you know because people want to see that you truly are an expert at what you do. How can you show them that that's the case if they haven't hired you? Give them the content they want before they've learned to trust you.

There are many reasons people binge-watch my channel when they discover me, and this is one of them. I don't keep my social media and video content marketing tips close to the vest. That does me no good. It's my job to teach you how to do my job. If I've done that, then I know I'm your trusted guide in this process. And the moment you need additional help or assistance that free videos cannot provide, I'm the one you'll come to.

Am I educating my competitors on how to do what I do? Yes. Are people copying me? Absolutely. I'm not making the content for them. My hope is that I do such a great job for Charlotte and everyone like her that they will continue to choose me over the rest. If they don't, and they choose a competitor, that's still my fault. No matter what you do (especially in the internet world), you must innovate. You must get better. You must be better. Most of all, you must stay focused on the whys and whos that really matter.

Stay focused and be generous. When you plan a video and deliver on these items, by the time you get to the end of the episode, your viewer will be ready to take action in addition to watching more episodes of your show.

Keep the Eyes Moving

Remember how I said people don't have a lot of time? Yeah, it's hard to keep someone's attention these days. The 8-Second Rule doesn't just apply to how long it will take someone to stay on your video, it's also the attention span of a human in 2016, falling from 12 seconds as documented in the year 2000. Basically, every 8 seconds you risk losing your viewer if you're not keeping them enthralled.

You're doing a great job so far. You brought them into the content quickly. You didn't waste time with branding. You've been generous with your content depth, and now you just gotta keep the eyes on the video.

Sounds easy, but even after doing all that work it can be a real challenge.

If their eyes are going to wander—maybe to check email or the latest text message—we want to give their eyes permission to wander within the walls of our video.

Think about the last movie you saw. You had your eyes on the screen for most of it if it was a good one, and the way directors do that is by cutting from one point of view to another every few moments. If it's a scene in which someone has a long monolog, you will still notice the camera angle changing often. It doesn't have to cut away. Maybe it just zooms in. It pulls you in by giving you a new and fresh perspective. Constantly.

Now think about a movie you saw 10 years ago. 20 years ago. If you try to watch that movie today, it's going to have a very different feel—longer. More artistic moments of non-movement. Longer stories. Longer lead-up to the big climax. You would get bored, if you were used to the pacing of today's content.

That's how you need to think about this video strategy. You can be like everyone else, taking the easy way out, just talking to a camera and uploading it directly. In some cases, that's going to work just fine. For the most part, you need to get creative in editing and filming to keep your viewer's attention when they're being pulled to find better entertainment every eight seconds.

If you have ever seen an episode of my show, you'll notice that one of the ways I do this is with an editing style called jump cutting. You literally never hear me breathe unless it's for comedic timing or the pacing is still on point. I'm going to get my message to you as quickly as possible by not allowing any downtime, feet shuffling, filler words or unnecessary pauses. No matter what.

This is an easy way to keep the eyes moving because the action of an abrupt cut in the footage is going to call attention back to the screen, especially when you don't hear someone breathing when they talk because it's been cut out. That's not natural. Therefore it calls attention.

I will also zoom in on my face during a funny moment or to drive a point home because that's going to ensure that the jump cuts are doing their job. The art of this cutting style is in the editing. It's easy to hammer out a great video quickly once you pick up the skill and get used to using a professional grade linear editor. If you would like to learn this editing technique, visit Vlog Boss University and take my micro-course at www.VlogBossUniversity.com.

Another tactic that helps with keeping eyes moving is integrating B-roll. If you're not sure what that is, think about your main video. Maybe it's you sitting in your office talking to the camera for five minutes. That video in its edited entirety is your A-roll. It's the main track of content that will be used for the video, and the audio will play a crucial role in pulling it together as well. B-roll is footage that cuts away from the person talking to focus on something else. (Only the visual changes; the A-roll audio continues to play.) So if the A-roll shows me talking to the camera about how to fold a paper airplane and I say, "Step one," I would then show B-roll of me going through the first step on a piece of paper as I keep talking. Changing up the perspective results in a more enhanced visual experience for the tutorial and also keeps your viewers' eyes moving (preventing boredom).

B-roll is essentially any visual you want to add to the experience while the main line of video keeps it together. It's the most effective way to keep the eyes moving while staying within your video experience.

Just like the A-roll can get boring, so too can the B-roll. Showing B-roll for too long is going to be boring to the eyes as well. Cutting back to the person talking again will be important.

For an idea on this, check out one of my videos from Savvy Sexy Social called 7 TIPS TO GET MORE DONE (http://savvysexysocial.com/getmoredone). This video is me listing seven productivity tips, but instead of relying on just naming them, I use visuals for B-roll to give you the perspective of how this tactic will help you.

This is a bit "in the weeds," as they say. The main thing you need to know is that the more perspectives you offer throughout the video, the more likely you're going to be able to hold on to your viewer until the end.

Don't let your viewer get bored. You're already delivering so much value, and you can't help but share it in the fast-moving age of information. If you want to hang in and win over your audience with video, you'll keep their eyes moving while keeping them square on your brand.

Save Time for the Close

We are in this video game to give value. Tons and tons and tons of value. It's the only way to get the attention we want and the best way to become the thought leaders of our industry.

When you give value, you have the ability to ask for some in return. That's the real beauty of content marketing. If you have done your job to deliver on what you said you would, and you've provided value to your audience, they will be waiting for you to tell them what to do next.

It's time for the close.

In the close of your video there needs to be a CTA as your return value. I'm going to talk about the specifics of that action call in the next section, but the key point I want to make here is that you need to make time for it.

I know that sounds like nonsense, right? "Of course I'm going to ask my viewers to do something for me at the end of the video!"

I'm sure you are. No doubt.

You need to be strategic in your *timing* of that close.

On one side of the spectrum, you have the people who go *all out* for the close.

It's easy for someone on camera to get into closing mode and just ramble on about what they would like for viewers to do and why. Some people feel there's something uncomfortable and "salesy" about asking for action, so they get a little wordy.

You should plan your close specifically and strategically, and that includes the timing.

For example, you do not want to create 2 minutes of valuable content and then spend 2 minutes on the close. First of all, you probably haven't earned the right to a 2-minute request. But the bigger problem is that you took a 2-minute video and made it a 4-minute video. The retention rate of viewers (the ratio of people still watching your video) is going to start dropping as soon as you reach the close. So for a video with 2 minutes of content, plan on a length of 30 seconds for a close. The 2-minute video is now a 2:30 video. That's not as big of a percentage, and therefore your audience retention (the percentage of the video that people watch) will be much higher.

Even if you're not as worried about audience retention as I think you should be, you should know that all CTAs are more effective when they are clear and concise. Don't wing it. Plan your close and stick to the talking points.

On the other end of the spectrum, you have quite the opposite issue: people who don't allocate any time for the close. They stay away from asking for any return whatsoever because they feel they did their job delivering great content, and they believe their viewers will automatically take action: visiting their website or following them on a social network.

Wrong. Your viewers will not do that. They will not do anything if you do not ask them to.

Obviously, there is a chance they could poke around. As sophisticated as these social networks are, they are more likely to click on the next suggested video or like another post than to visit your website when you didn't tell them.

Don't be the video creator who is constantly giving value and never asking for anything in return. It will make the request even harder when you finally start integrating it into your content.

Think about how long this video is going to be. How much time do you need to explain the CTA? You need to plan for somewhere around 15 seconds to a minute. A minute-long CTA is more appropriate for a longer video (5 minutes or more). But just because you have a long video doesn't mean the action call needs to be long. It just depends on the context of the video content and the relativity of the request. If the content was amazing and something people would pay for, this is an opportunity for a bigger, more needle-moving request that might take more time to explain.

Make the time. Plan for it. Ask.

Also, I'd like to make an important distinction here. You do not automatically get anything from your viewers just because you made a video. All this does is give you more authority to *ask* for a return. We do not give, and give, and give, then receive. We give, and give, and give, so we can request. Remember how precious your viewers' attention is, and keep that in mind when you close.

Audible and Clear Call to Action

Now that you know how much time you need to allow for your call to action, let's talk about how to make it effective.

As I said before, not planning this part can cause you to wing it and make the action call more confusing than it needs to be.

First and foremost, clarity starts with an audible action call. In video, we have the luxury of both audio and visual. If you do not leverage both, you lose some effectiveness. This is especially true for the CTA.

You can put a pretty graphic on-screen saying, "Subscribe to our YouTube channel!" but if you don't say it out loud, it's significantly less likely to happen. People see ads and graphics and words on their devices All The *Time*. If you want yours to be special, you have to say it.

The crazy thing is that if you actually kept someone's attention for this entire piece of content and they've been listening to you the whole time, all you have to do is say a CTA, and they will want to take it. The audible action is the one taken.

Your description section will be useful. Your graphics and editing will make it look professional. You *must* say it. Don't just display it.

Now that you understand the need for an audible request, we need it to be as clear as possible so viewers will take action.

The first important point about clarity in a CTA is to make it relative to the video experience. Just because you made one video that taught someone how to bake a cake doesn't mean that at the end of the video they are ready to whip out their credit card and reserve you as their private chef. That isn't realistic. You have to give a ton of value to win over your potential clients, and that one piece of content isn't going to cut it. (No pun intended.)

They might, however, decide you are a YouTube channel worth subscribing to for more baked goodness. That would be an excellent example of relative return. "Thank you for watching! If you enjoyed this and would like to help me continue making these videos for free, please click the subscribe button. You will receive an update when my next video arrives!" Easy. Simple. This is a great reason for the viewer to take action. It's very relative to their video experience.

If you're hoping to do more than build your social following and contribute to something that will help you boost your bottom line, that can still be relative as well. For the majority of my career, my CTAs focused on getting people to join my email list (rather than the typical "subscribe to my YouTube channel") so I could connect with them directly in their inbox.

Just joining an email list isn't going to be very enticing for anyone, but you can offer an incentive. Let's say that the cake-baking video's goal is to connect via email with viewers who might eventually like to buy a cookbook. It is crucial to

> People like having choices, but when faced with too many, they get paralyzed in the choosing process.

create a CTA that is relevant to the fact that the viewers want to learn about baking. As an incentive to join an email list, the creator could offer a free gift that would be delivered automatically by email marketing software, like *The Baking Basics Checklist for Your Home Kitchen*, a list of tools and pantry items that would be helpful for bakers to always have on hand.

Think about that process. Person searches how to bake a cake. Person watches your video on how to bake a cake. Person gets to end of video where you are their baking thought leader who just taught them how to bake a cake. Thought leader suggests that they should also have this checklist to make sure they're covered for their future baking needs.

It's a fitting, relative, and even valuable CTA that falls in line with the viewer's immediate goals. Now they're on an email list which is an incredible place to connect directly with consumers who are making buying decisions regularly. (Email marketing is not dead, people! It's a big deal for your bottom line.)

That is an example of clear and relative return. How can you make it easy to follow your brand? Make it too valuable to pass up.

The final important point about the CTA is that you must keep it *clear*. One of the traps that people fall into is asking for too many things. Asking for all the things means you will likely get nothing.

"Subscribe to this YouTube channel, and download this free PDF! Make sure you call us if you have any questions or want to hire us. Oh, and follow on Twitter because, why not?!"

Too. Many. Things.

These days, people love choices. At least they think they do. People like having choices, but when faced with too many, they get paralyzed in the choosing process. It's just a fact. That's why when you look at modern website design, the best sites are the ones with very little for you to do and minimalist layouts. If you want someone to do one thing, don't give them 50 million other things to click on that would distract from that one thing.

The same is true for your CTA. Make it simple and easy so you can track how well you're converting a viewer into an action taker. No matter what that action is.

Be clear and say what you want people to do. Your content has earned you the right to ask. If you delivered on what you promised, you will probably find that your viewers want to take the next step.

Length of Video

You've done a lot of planning for every second of your video up to this point. Now we're going to wrap it all up with a beautiful bow.

The length of your video is critical. We are transitioning into a world of longer-form content, and shorter-the-better no longer reigns supreme. However, when you are an unknown brand and just getting started, you don't have a lot of time to waste. I've harped on that quite a bit.

That is why, in my Authority Video Formula, I recommend a video's final timestamp to be somewhere in the neighborhood of two to five minutes.

This also depends on what the video is about. If you're doing that cake baking tutorial, maybe it will take a little longer. With the power of editing, and for the sake of keeping the eyes moving, do you really need longer than five minutes? Even the baking shows on TV that have an hour of programming go over a recipe wicked fast, thankfully, because of pre-prepared steps in the process. You don't have to wait for results.

The best way to figure out the ideal length of your video is to look up your competition. What comes up on the front page of search results for this kind of content? If there are other videos with the same subject, how long did it take them to get the message across?

Let's say you end up on the front page of search results for your video. Your competitor's result is there offering a cake baking tutorial in two minutes, and yours takes seven. Who do you think is going to win over the heart of the busy mom trying to give her kid the best birthday ever?

Yup. Two minutes, please.

It's not all about competition, but those opportunities to have an edge might be clear as day if you just do a little research.

Another reason I like shorter videos is that they keep you focused on what you're talking about. This will make your headline and search rankings more specific, targeting your perfect viewer.

On YouTube, there is another metric you should be thinking about in your analytics that will help you build rapport as an effective channel: watch time.

YouTube Watch time is your ability as a creator to bring viewers onto the YouTube platform and keep them watching. This may or may not even mean your own content! The goal of YouTube is to get people to watch a video and then watch about a million more. In 2016, the average viewer in a mobile viewing session watched YouTube for 40 minutes. That's a *long* time. Good news for long-form content, but only if it's good enough to keep people there. It's actually great news for short-form content because if you deliver quickly and efficiently, you will make the viewer want more. YouTube likes that.

Bringing people in and getting that view and those minutes watched on your video is a start. When they stay logged into YouTube longer because of your video (whether they keep watching your content or move to someone else's), then you are making YouTube happy. You kicked off that viewer's session, and therefore the rest of their session is going to reflect on you positively or negatively. All of these factors have to do with your watch time and will let YouTube know how they should reward you in search and referral traffic.

On Facebook, you may not want to take this advice at all. If the views are happening in a disruptive way (your video started playing automatically on someone's News Feed), the viewers are hard to impress. Viewing on Facebook can go on for two to five minutes, but you may only have three seconds of video to get their attention. As I've said before, if you don't do something visually compelling to bring them into your video and stop scrolling in the first place, the video length doesn't even matter.

The bottom line is that there are plenty of video creators who are successful with one-minute videos and plenty who are successful with 60-minute videos. You need to think about your viewer and what they want. How does it fit into their life? How much time do they have for this? Fit your strategy to that mold and then look up your competition to verify your chances of winning viewers in search and social feeds.

When no one knows who you are, the value is all that matters. Therefore the focus should be on delivering, calling action, and then moving on.

One More Thing

Hopefully, this formula has given you confidence, and you're amped and excited to create your first video.

Sometimes all we need is some structure and guidance on how to attack the project ahead of us.

Before closing this chapter, I want to go over an incredibly important element of vlogging success. It has to do with the actual filming, your on-camera presence.

Success with video starts with the personable approach of your face on a screen, but *that's not enough.* The audience needs a deeper connection to you, or else this is all for naught.

The most critical component of vlogging is how you look into that camera lens. It doesn't matter what camera you have. It doesn't matter if you're making your first or 1,000th video. It doesn't matter how many followers you do or don't have.

You will only win with video if you look at the camera like it is a person.

Period.

We designed your viewer persona for this very reason. They will inspire everything you do. Your goal is to always keep that person in mind when vlogging so you'll make the best possible product for them every time.

Envision their face. Know their struggle. Understand their current situation. Even think their name (the one you gave them). These are the things you must focus on when you talk to the camera because that's what customizes the experience for your perfect viewer. It's what makes them feel more connected to you—like you're in the same room together.

Talk to the lens like you're speaking to your perfect viewer. When you do, you'll find there are many more than one to serve. They will show up as the most incredible community you could ever imagine!

Your Fabulous Formula

As I've stressed, this formula is not going to be the perfect fit for every scenario. However, if you choose to follow its guidance, you'll be arming yourself with an incredible execution style. Getting started in video is hard enough for so many reasons. An effective strategy for each piece of content will help you enormously.

Take this formula into consideration when you're planning your first videos. Know that you've given the best possible presentation to your audience.

CHAPTER EIGHT
KILLER COLLABORATION

If your brand has competitors, think about who they are. Are they creating video content? If they are, that's not surprising, but there probably aren't many of them. Either way, is the content any good?

I don't believe in competition against anyone, except my former self. Every day, it's my job to be better than yesterday's Amy. I'm the only person I can control going forward, so I can't worry about others being better or worse than me. We don't all have the same circumstances, mindset, drive, ambition, or anything else that matters. We're all different, and we can all be an authority in our own right.

This isn't something I want to harp on much here, but I feel it's an important thing to address because so many people think competitively. It's not that I'm not competitive, because I am. I just want to encourage you to think outside of that, because so much of video success comes from collaboration, not competition.

One of my longtime friends in the YouTube space is Austin Evans. He is a tech review video producer, and there are a lot of other people doing something similar. Rather than thinking of them as competition, Austin and many others in this space see great value in working together. There are always going to be more viewers, subscribers, and money to go around. Instead of competing, the people in this community come together to cross-promote and spread around a similar audience to benefit many hard working creators.

Each of them is unique anyway. Some of them are extremely funny. Others like to be more serious and insert small bouts of dry humor. Some specialize in unboxing new technology while others focus more on reporting the latest news. Everyone's target audience has a similar interest. When they learn about new channels that offer an interesting take on the content they already love, it helps everyone involved.

I met Austin when he had a highly impressive YouTube channel of 30,000 subscribers. Today he's amassed nearly 2 million, and while quality and consistency played an important role, a great deal of credit goes to the collaborative partnerships he has created. He even moved from his home in the middle of America to Los Angeles to be more accessible for collaborative and business opportunities.

This might not be something everyone can do. As much as I've always felt the pressure to move to New York or LA, Columbus is my home. I choose to be here and deal with some of those consequences. No matter where you're based or what your content is, there is always a way to collaborate and increase your brand awareness.

Collaboration can take many different forms and might be possible remotely as well as in person.

Now that you're clear about the content you want to create and the audience who will appreciate it, let's talk about how you can collaborate (or "collab", as we say in the industry) to grow exponentially with video.

Teaming Up

Do you know how incredible it is to be able to say you have the trust of an audience? Knowing it, feeling it, having the ability to sell yourself because of it... it's huge. Everything you do in every video you create affects the significance of your influence and rapport with your viewer.

The results are never greater than when a true collaboration happens.

Let's talk about what it is first. Collaboration, as it is most often referred to in the field of content creation, is when one brand/person/influencer and another brand/person/influencer come together to create. Creator A makes a video on his or her own video channel and invites Creator B to be featured in the content. A lot of times it will happen the other way around in the same video creation session: Creator B will make a video for their own presence and feature Creator A.

It sounds simple. It is. Very, very simple. The reason it can make such an incredible difference in your video presence is the clout you have with your audience.

They trust you. They know you're only going to share things that matter to you the most, information that is pertinent, and, in this case, the people that you believe your audience should know.

This is why collaboration is a huge opportunity for you to get in front of a new audience. That audience already has a social authority offering them content, and when that authority teams up with you, that is instant social proof. The new audience automatically has a reason to trust you.

Even though collaboration happens often and doesn't surprise viewers, it's still amazing how powerful it is. When people are engaged in your content and love everything you're doing, they want to live vicariously and meet new people through you. When you feature someone in your video and make them relevant to your community, your audience has a chance to form a relationship with them as well.

Because of this strategy, this is—far and away—the reason creators grow exponentially in reach and community size. Viral videos can do it too but who's banking on that? I would rather have someone find me as a personal recommendation from someone they trust than have them stumble upon a video that happens to be getting a lot of traction. My video would only satisfy them for a fleeting moment.

If you're just getting started, it may feel like collaboration is a long way off for you right now. The misconception that you need social media numbers to prove your worth and make a video collaboration happen needs to stop here. You need to collaborate as soon as possible. It cannot wait for you to reach some arbitrary number that will give you a potential platform to approach another creator.

We all have something we can do for others. When we go into these proposals with that mentality, it's more likely we can make it happen. You may not have a subscriber count to propose, but what do you have? Could you take on a project that would otherwise cost the person money? Is there something you've done for them in the past that could potentially be leveraged for a favor?

There are a lot of ways to think about this, and I encourage you to think outside of the box to help yourself reach a larger audience. It doesn't have to be a follow-ers-to-followers comparison.

When it is, there's something else to keep in mind. Just because someone has the same number of subscribers as you doesn't mean they're

> Don't be disrespectful thinking that someone seems so nice that they owe you something. They don't.

automatically a good fit. Nope. Not a real thing. Also, I hope it goes without saying that if you follow someone with a million subscribers and you're just getting started, reaching out to them with nothing comparable to offer would be a waste of time.

Not just a waste of your time. A waste of their time. Don't be disrespectful thinking that someone seems so nice that they owe you something. They don't.

This is meant to be fun. It's meant to be collaborative. It's meant to spread the love. That doesn't mean people don't treat this like a business (especially when we're talking about something so huge as giving you the social proof of introducing you to their trusting community).

You have to get outside of your usual box to find these collaborative opportunities. It might not be someone you've even watched before. We're going to get into search engine optimization (or "SEO") research later, and one of the things we'll talk about is YouTube search. Why don't you go ahead and dive in? Think about some of the videos you want to create in the future and find out who is already showing up for those subjects. What do those channels look like? Are they growing a similar audience to the one you want to target? Look at their comments and dig into what people are saying. Look at names and profiles to learn more about them.

The research on this side is huge, because it will equip you to go to a channel that may not have any idea who you are but would be interested in collaborating if you presented it the right way. Knowing their audience really well is a great way to impress right off the bat.

When I say proposal, I mean it. Maybe you'll get lucky if you reach out and say something like, "Let's collaborate!" but in most cases, you will be taken more seriously if you let the person know exactly what you'd like to do with them and why both of your audiences will love it.

For example, let's say our Cooking Channel friend wants to reach out to another channel to collaborate. The Cooking Channel has grown to about 10,000 subscribers on YouTube. She sees another channel that has the same number of subscribers and publishes videos about how to live well economically as a family.

If the Cooking Channel were super savvy and wanted to reach out to the Living Well Family channel, here's a great approach:

1. Send a tweet or leave a comment asking for contact information to propose a collaboration (or skip a step by finding the business email in the LWF channel's About section). Next, send a brief email—and I mean brief—telling who she is and the idea that they could work together to spread the audience love across channels. (The introduction of who you are and what your channel is about should be one or two sentences max. We don't want potential collaborators to get bored and never read the part of the email about the collaboration.)

2. Propose a two-video cross-promotional collaboration. One video is for the Cooking Channel about how to find the best deals on ingredients at the grocery store, featuring the advice of the guest expert: the LWF channel. The second video

is for the LWF channel about how to prepare a delicious and impressive Thanksgiving dinner for under $100, featuring the guest expert: the Cooking Channel. Both videos will be published at the same time, promoting both channels, and asking viewers to navigate to the visiting channel to subscribe.

3. Ask the LWF channel to reply with thoughts on the idea. Ask about their availability. Say that she's flexible if the other channel already has a plan like this in production (make sure to do homework on what videos they've already done recently that shouldn't be too closely repeated).

Reaching out with a plan and the clear steps to make a collaboration happen is the most effective way to get a person to work with you. They can always turn you down, but at least it wasn't for lack of preparation. It may just not be a good fit for them right now. If they don't write back, follow up once. Creators tend to get a lot of viewer emails, and you are technically a viewer until you step up to become a collaboration partner.

It doesn't need to be this structured every time. It just depends on how well you know the person or how interested you think they might be based on their social activity and history of working with others. Going into the conversation putting a lot of responsibility on another channel to come up with an idea is a sure way to get shrugged off and lose an opportunity, especially when making a first impression.

Do your research. Understand their content strategy. Read their audience. Create your proposal and put it out there. The worst that could happen is a no. The best that could happen is a plan in motion.

The Travel Collab

So everyone you want to work with is nowhere near you geographically? I feel ya. As I mentioned, it's easy to feel the pressure to move, but the truth is that you can still collaborate without uprooting your home. I should know, as stubborn and proud as I am to be a resident of my hometown, Columbus.

First, if you want to do a lot of in-person collaborations, that's totally acceptable. They are probably the most fun and interesting for creators and viewers alike. Maybe there is a city with quite a few collaboration opportunities stacking up. Think about how much you could do if you made a special trip to that location just to create some great content!

As this platform becomes more like a business to you (if it isn't already), something like this makes a lot of sense. It's similar to how you would attend a conference in your industry to meet new people and think of ways you can work with them. Making the investment in a productive visit is a massively good idea.

You might be hesitant about this. You wouldn't want to post a bunch of collaborations one after the other. Maybe you want to make sure your audience remembers the main purpose of the channel, or, more importantly, you may have only designated one bucket per month as a collaboration opportunity. Good for you! This is a great mindset to have.

When I travel and knock out a few videos at once, my preference is to not let the excitement get to me and still schedule them accordingly. Remember: context is everything. If the video is timely and relevant at this moment, maybe it needs to go out. If it's evergreen (meaning the content is perpetually relevant), then it can wait for the next time you're ready to post a bigger event like this.

Collaborations are just that: events. These are pillars for your video channel and need the regular programming in between to string everything together effectively. Travel to create four videos and think about where they will ultimately end up on your programming calendar. Even if it's August right now, you could collaborate with someone on a Christmas project.

Making a trip to collaborate with several people at once and scheduling the content for the future is a great idea for fitting collaboration into your strategy. I like conserving eventful pillar content so that you don't go through a collaboration dry spell if you can't travel all the time.

Start thinking about what cities you'll visit and how you can find people to collaborate with. Make those arrangements quickly. Or, if you're going to plan a trip down the road, start making connections now. Taking this seriously will be a major advantage when reaching out.

But being in-person isn't the only way. So let's talk about additional options for collaborating that allow you to stay put.

The Remote Collab

Many times have I leveraged the remote collab. Just because you're not in the same room doesn't mean you can't have the same effect as a team. Let's look at the ways you can propose a collaboration while staying in your own studio.

The beauty of the internet is that we're able to create videos, upload them, share them, and edit our footage together with someone else. Lots of parodies are built on this ability. You can use the same concept for remote collaboration.

The goal is simply to get both of you on-screen together. That's it. Technology makes that easy. Your collaboration proposal only changes because of the logistics of how it will be filmed to accommodate for not being in the same room together.

It's important to remember the context of the channel for your viewers. They trust you. If you disappear for some reason and another person pops on without you, the collab may not be well received.

If you were thinking that maybe you'd both just create videos for each other's channels, I would advise—slightly—against that. In my experience (so that you don't completely throw your audience for a loop), it would be best if you're both in the video, but the clips can be stitched together in the editing phase.

I love a good channel takeover, but I want to see the face of the creator I trust before someone unexpected is thrust onto the scene.

A couple of examples of this are on my channel. I love giving a smaller creator a chance to share their advice with my community (if I've seen their stuff and it's a fit in content and delivery). In those cases, I asked the creator to send me a completed video (edited and ready to publish) that was strictly the meat of the content. No crazy long introductions or calls to action. That's my job. For those videos, I filmed an introduction welcoming my viewers to the video and letting them know I invited someone to share their great content. Then I cut in the footage that my collaborative partner sent me for the next section of the video. I also filmed an outro to follow that section to let people know what they should do next, like subscribe to the featured creator and/or leave a comment regarding the subject matter of the video.

Another idea is to not worry about being in each other's videos at all, and just give them a shout-out. Let's say the

Cooking Channel is going to publish a video about how to pack affordable, but awesome, lunches for the first week back to school. The channel would proceed with the video as usual but choose to include footage and a shout-out to the Living Well Family channel we mentioned earlier. Perhaps they have a video they're posting about best affordable back-to-school finds. The themes align, and both channels give a shout-out to the other video to offer a cross-promotion opportunity.

A great example of this is a collaboration I did with my friend Stephanie Carls. Not only did we give each other a shout-out in our videos, but we aligned them to be relevant on a fun holiday. On Fight Procrastination Day we each agreed to upload a video with our three favorite apps to fight procrastination. I focused on iPhone apps. She focused on Android. We swapped a little footage to be featured in each other's content while encouraging viewers to watch the other video. You can watch the videos from this collaboration on www.VlogBossUniversity.com.

The key here is uploading at the same time and making sure you're on the same page logistically. It's no fun for one person to do this when the other video isn't ready yet. When done correctly, it can be effective for a more relaxed referral. Baking a referral into the content is important. It's more likely to convert a referred viewer than just linking to it in the description without a mention in the content itself. Give them a taste of the other channel in the content they're already watching, and they're more likely to make a move if it aligns with their current interests. (Hence, the necessity for a similar theme.)

This is the best way to get around geographic constraints. The example I described is pretty cut and dried, but you could easily do something similar with a scripted sketch or list of ideas. The listicle is particularly fun because you can get many creators into one video, similar to what I did for my 500th episode. I emailed many different people (not just YouTubers) to send me a video clip of them talking about what they thought made a brand Savvy, Sexy, and Social. Then I edited them together to offer my community a montage of great people who have enjoyed watching my channel and have also learned something from it. Check out the final product to see what a giant remote collaboration looks like on www.VlogBossUniversity.com.

There are so many examples of things you can do remotely to work together. Get inspired. Watch videos. See what others are doing. Figure out what you can do virtually versus what would be best in person. There are probably more opportunities than you think to get creative and make an impact with cross-promotion.

We are using the internet. The possibilities for success are endless, anywhere in the world.

The Sneaky Collab

Did you know that you can collab with someone without them even knowing it? It's one of the most popular tactics in online video brand awareness. All you need to do is associate yourself with another person or brand through your content. This can be as fruitful as a collaboration effort that you orchestrated directly with them.

I'll give you a great example. Remember the first story I told you about my music video for Gary Vaynerchuk? The #1 question I get about that video is, "How did you arrange your video with Gary and his team? How did he help you or play a role?"

Gary? He didn't know a thing about it! Remember when I said I was simply hoping he would see an email or tweet? Yeah. Pretty strong indication he didn't even know it was happening. He knew I was going to review his book like everyone else, but that's about it. Nothing strong enough for a tick on the radar.

I created that video and associated myself with his brand. I was fortunate that he saw the content, enjoyed it, and then shared it with his community because that elevated the collaboration opportunity. I didn't need to ask his permission or arrange for him to appear in my video to make it happen. As a matter of fact, years later when he asked me to do another music video for his second book, he still wasn't a partner in that effort. I did it all on my own, though this time it was different: I knew I could get on his radar more easily.

Think bigger about collaboration. If you feel defeated about needing to reach out to people to arrange some big event between your two channels, think about how you can collaborate with others without having to bug them about it in the process. You can often achieve similar benefits, especially if the other person happens to enjoy what you did and shares it with their community.

Collaboration Calls to Action

If you're doing all this planning to work with a collaborative partner, you want to make sure all your effort pays off. You need a call to action. Covering your bases with a few best practices is key.

One CTA is obvious: encourage new subscribers. Typically, when you see someone new appear on a channel, the goal is to have viewers move over and subscribe to their channel. If you don't say that out loud, though, viewers may not even think about it!

Calling out to your own subscribers on your own content to subscribe to the person who is being featured in the video goes a long way. It also goes hand-in-hand with the idea of lending your trust to that person. You must personally recommend them to your audience, or they won't do anything out of the ordinary.

The collaborators who want to get the most out of a CTA will incorporate a giveaway opportunity for their community. For instance, maybe both creators go in on a nice gift like an iPad to give away to one lucky viewer. To enter, all they have to do is make sure they're subscribed to both of the participating channels and leave a comment for tracking purposes.

Something to note, especially on YouTube, is that you can't track who your subscribers are in a sophisticated fashion (at least not at the moment). So when you say, "You must be subscribed to both of our channels for a chance to win," you're relying on the honor system here. Could you technically award someone who wasn't subscribed to one or both channels? Sure, but because both followings will be aggressively subscribing to ensure their best chance to win, the creators still achieve what they want out of it: a growing following and new people seeing their content.

I'm not sure if this is some best-kept YouTube secret or if it's clearly obvious to everyone, but I always found it interesting that it works this way. Keywords being: it works.

On that note, from a giveaway perspective, maybe you do want to take a chance on a channel which is a little bit bigger to offer a collaboration. Including a giveaway and taking on the responsibility of buying and managing the giveaway might give you a leg up. You still need to do your homework on the channel to see if this will be a good fit and if the giveaway item is appropriate. They might want to do a video that shows off how giving they are (even if you're the one buying the product for their audience). So why not facilitate that?

Obviously, you need to analyze what the potential return of the collaboration would be and if that dollar amount is going to be worth it for you. You can't guarantee a result. Certainly, the creator you're proposing to work with won't be able to either. If you think about what success would look like and how much you're willing to pay for it, the giveaway offer for collaboration is a great opportunity to get a higher rate of return.

Will they subscribe to you if you collaborate without a giveaway? Sure, but incentive will always get you greater results. It's up to you to analyze how to make the most of any opportunity.

Another big tip here is that engagement is huge. Making sure you reap the benefits doesn't end when the collab goes live. You must join the conversation. If you want to see people become interested in you after they see you in their favorite channel's video, chat with them in the comments on that video and in others. This will make a big impact that will make the average viewer want to get to know you even better and subscribe for future content.

There are going to be many other types of CTAs that are going to be important for your collaborative effort. Just remember that this is not an afterthought. It needs to be recognized and organized from the beginning as you start to develop a plan for your collaboration project. Get focused on the return you want to see, decide on appropriate CTAs, and then shape a proposal to work with other creators who are interested in growing their presences as well.

CHAPTER NINE
ELECTRIFYING ENGAGEMENT

Too often we hear people stress out over their lack of engagement online. Whether it's tweets without conversation or a YouTube video with no comments, no engagement can be a little depressing.

But guess what? It's your fault.

That wasn't meant to hurt, but maybe it did. The reality is that you can't just sit on what you've created based on the "if you build it, they will come" mentality. It just doesn't work that way. Actually, I can't think of a great example where that is true, because it's not just online media where this policy does not work. It's pretty much everywhere.

You can have the best product ever—even better than existing competition—but if no one knows about it because you didn't market it correctly, it might as well not even exist.

Engagement works the same way. You have to create the content. Then you have to let people know that content exists. *Then* you need to encourage people to think about what they should do next.

If they watched your video or arrived at your content at all, they are now looking to you as their leader to tell them what to do with the knowledge or information they just acquired from you. So, do tell. What do you want them to do?

You can't get upset about people not commenting or sharing enough if you didn't make it explicitly clear that they should do so.

Great example: men. We think they know a lot. Maybe they do. However, they don't usually know a lot about what women want, because we keep the unsaid thing in our heads and assume that putting out a "vibe" will be enough.

Viewers are like men. They don't get it. You have to tell them explicitly.

Sorry to all the viewers who are also men. At least you're consistent.

Women viewers, it's okay. We can't guess what a creator wants us to do, so we move on to the next thing. We're busy. Naturally.

Bottom line: if you want comments, *ask*. If you want shares, *ask*. If you want an answer to a question about what's going on in the heads of your viewers, *ask*. They're only listening to every word you have to say, so why would you waver on the thing that's going to help you grow this creative operation? Results mean engagement. Engagement means action. You must instruct the action to get engagement and therefore results.

Let's go into a few forms of engagement that you might need to focus on, beginning with the most sensitive and extensive topic: the comments section.

YouTube Comments

One of the reasons YouTube has become so infamous is their comments section. People often think that if you want to get depressed, you should read the comments section of a YouTube video.

It's true. It can be a little depressing. Until you remember that we are not simply putting billboards up anymore. The person with the most money for a commercial is not the only one who can attract brand attention. The internet and social media have completely changed the way we communicate. People can have a say from their computers at home in the comments, just like anyone can now share their opinion and ideas with the world by starting a blog.

The thing I've always kept in mind in this aspect of content creation is that most people are good. Truly. The bad eggs are usually not your target audience or customer, but if they are you can watch for a trend of negativity to know when you're truly in the wrong. Most of the time, you're not.

I've had the great fortune of having an enviable You-Tube comments section where—at least in the first two to five days of a video—the comments are 98% positive. I think there are a lot of tactics that have contributed to that which I want to share with you here. But I also don't want to come into this being all sunshine and rainbows.

To prep for this section of the book, yesterday I posted a video that was unusual for my channel, a video with some uncensored motivational opinion. I'm known as a "tactics and tips" kind of channel, but that's only going to get you so far in the world of video. Once you've built an audience of people who trust you, I believe it's important to continue to keep content fresh for them and also let them see more of you—how you think, how you feel.

The video was about why your idea isn't special, the main takeaway being that you can make it special by simply taking action. If you rely too much on what other people tell you, like friends and family who are trying to lift you up, then you'll get into trouble. You can't base your worth on an idea that "everyone says is great!"

This morning, I spent an hour going through the comments and tweets from the video a little less than 12 hours from publishing. The call to action was to post a comment with how you're taking action on your idea today now that I've motivated you to stop just thinking about it.

The comments were 98% positive and excited, but the 2% popped up a little early this time to tell me they didn't appreciate the video.

Perfect. Now I'm ready to write this section of the book.

Let's start with the high percentage of positive comments. This is different, and it's not the average scenario in videos for a few reasons.

1) Your Niche Affects Everything. Especially Your Comments.

I think where a lot of videos get into trouble with a higher ratio of negativity is when they are a channel trying to be all things to all people. When you do not niche down enough, you can open yourself up to a much larger audience of people who shouldn't necessarily be there.

I recently clicked on a video that was a list of life hacks which, according to the title, "*everyone* needs to know." The thumbnail was well done, very feminine, with "life hacks" printed on top of an image of one of the hacks. It was incredibly inviting, and I considered myself a member of the "everyone" crowd. At least the crowd of everyone who wanted more hacks for a better life.

This video was one of the hardest videos I've ever had to watch. Not only were the tips subpar, but she also seemed very unprepared and didn't deliver on her promise. It even listed things that are probably illegal and had no proof or research on her end to the contrary. You can't tell people to hack their life by doing something illegal. Or can you?

This was a professional YouTube creator with close to 300,000 subscribers and more than six million views on this video. I have had an easier time watching my clients' first videos. It was dreadful.

Much to my lack of surprise, the comments followed suit, with one person chiming in, "This video is cancer," which had been voted up to the top by the majority of other users. Yikes. Who wants that as the top comment on their video? I wouldn't even wish this on Life-Hack-Girl.

This is a prime example of trying to reach the masses and getting every consequence that comes with it, good and bad. The good? It's lucrative. That video is likely bringing in a decent chunk of change from Google AdSense, and that's very obviously the point. The more eyeballs, the more profitable your content on YouTube. But you also either need to have a thick skin to deal with how people are receiving your work or, better yet, not look at the comments at all. Because that was more painful than the video itself.

I don't know about you, but I'm creating content to help people. I want to make them happy that they can change their lives and accomplish something amazing. I want them to watch my content and be able to go out and do something. Immediately. The comments are an important reflection of whether I've done my job or not. I can't do a crappy video just because it might go mainstream if it means my community will suffer.

2) People Don't Talk Crap (As Much) When You're in the Room.

I credit a lot of my success in the comments section to this one, but it's not because I was trying to avoid negative comments. I honestly didn't know any better.

At the beginning, I think we're all similar in how we upload a video to YouTube. That video goes live, we do whatever we can to promote it. Then we sit, watch, and wait for any action in views whatsoever.

Well, that was certainly a habit I was in, and I still am to this day. I think you should spend more time promoting a video than you did creating it. I also think watching for the activity in those first moments is important.

As we've discussed already, the first 48 hours are crucial. The effects in those first couple days that matter are more than just outside in, meaning how many views and commenters are engaging the video. They are also inside out, as in what you as the creator decide to do to keep up this conversation.

Chiming in with your viewers in the comments has a massive payoff. First, you're going to get more views and comments from your audience because the amount of interaction shows YouTube that it is an engaging video worth spreading to a larger audience.

But even better, you're showing your audience that you don't just drop the mic when you share your ideas in a video. You're going to continue to talk with them and exchange ideas. That's all I was doing at the beginning. If I got a comment, I was going to reply. I replied to every comment on my videos.

It was easy at first, because I might get just one. But hey, if I replied, I had two comments on that video. That's double! As more and more trickled in, it was just second nature for me to keep chatting with as many people as I could. After all, I invited them to my little area of the internet to watch my content. How could I bail on them now?

Everyone knew I would be there. They saw my name along with theirs in the comments, and they knew I had a presence. Do you know how much more thoughtful and intentional those comments are when people know you're going to read them? That comment then becomes a new responsibility, not just a spew of words into the ether. The culture is completely different.

Now, as I said, I prepped for this section of the book by intentionally sitting down and replying to comments (every last one) for a video that was not my norm and a little controversial. So, of course, I had some negativity or passive aggressive

> Usually, the people who are negative are the ones who don't know me.

tendencies pop up in the comments. And, of course, I have received other negative comments in the past as well. They happen.

What I've noticed about these people is that when they pop up, I have never seen their name before. Usually, because they don't even have a photo uploaded to their avatar and are going by a fake name. Those are good reasons not to worry about those people in the least.

For those people who haven't shown up in the past, but are writing criticism next to their name and photo, I know that the video was not right for this stage of our relationship. Maybe they just met me and haven't bought in yet. My approach to motivation isn't sunshine and rainbows, so if it's not a day they're willing to take the heat, it's not our day. If the case is that they're showing their face and name, but saying something entirely uncalled-for, I'm not going to become part of their drama. I just have to know that this sort of thing happens. There's not much I can do about it.

Usually, the people who are negative are the ones who don't know me. They don't know how much I care and didn't bother to research before they let whatever is bugging them motivate a negative post on the internet. My video just happened to be where they stopped to do it. Could happen to anyone.

You learn to deal with those things, especially when you are so fortunate as to have built a culture of people who want to have a real conversation with you. You have done the work to facilitate it. People don't talk crap about Mama when she's in the room. Be in the room. Be present. You will be much better off in the long run.

Sure, there's a point of critical mass where this might feel or become less true. Cross that bridge when you come to it. Don't write off your early adopters just because you know that, on a grand scale, it can't be this easy. I guarantee you'll never get there unless you show the love your audience deserves from the beginning.

3) You Can't Just Win People Over with Your Headlines. You Must Deliver on Content as Well.

There was a time on YouTube when you could just name your video something—anything. YouTube would believe you were talking about said topic and help you rank in search accordingly. Those days are long gone.

The engagement side of YouTube helps them police people who do not deliver on the content they are promising.

Now, if you're reading this book, you're probably not one of those people who plans to put "JUSTIN BIEBER SONG LEAK" in your title only to disappoint people with what you're really sharing (this is commonly known as *clickbait*). That's an extreme example of why engagement on YouTube is so important. They need help finding the bad eggs. Users help make that happen by identifying the videos and/or channels that need to be removed.

However, this is where things get interesting. Remember when I told you about the terrible video a little earlier that might have been the worst list of life hacks in history? Well, engagement helped her in that case, good and bad.

That's because any comments and ratings on your video (thumbs up/thumbs down) are positive reflections of your video. Yes. Thumbs down can be positive video engagement as long as you made good on your promise. It shows YouTube that there is some engagement and activity. Even if everyone is saying in the comments that your work is terrible, it's a piece of content that is getting attention. Google/YouTube sees an opportunity to make money with it. The amount of negativity is a red flag for them to double-check the video. If the creator didn't lie about what they were sharing, it's fair game.

This is where comments can get really depressing, all because you didn't quite do the job. What starts as just your immediate community expressing their dissatisfaction is going to grow exponentially. People are more vocal about something they're upset about than something they like, so the engagement will be higher. YouTube sees that this video is kickin' with engagement, so they will get you more traction in referral traffic and search results. This will send more people who may be disappointed with what they watch. The negativity piles up.

You have to ask yourself, is it worth it? All this attention is negative in the eyes of your viewers but positive in the algorithms of search. One thing is for sure: if you're someone who cares about continuing the conversation in the comments, this will be a rough one. We need to talk about covering your bases for all video commentary in the future.

A Comment Policy

No matter how big or small your brand presence is online, you should have a comment policy. For inspiration, think about all the big companies that have to reply to dissatisfied customers via social media. They know they're going to be talked about, good or bad, and they have standard wording lined up to customize a response for each occasion.

This is something you need as well. You don't need the same canned response every time (actually, that is exactly what you *don't* need), but it would be good for you to have guidelines for how you handle different situations.

Positive Comments

Positivity is easy. Proceed with a response that continues the lovefest and leaves you and the commenter feeling uplifted and excited about your work.

Constructive Criticism

Constructive criticism sounds good, but sometimes we can get on the defensive if we didn't want it or aren't in the mood to take it. Trust me when I say that I'm one of the first people to screw this one up. I truly don't want to, because this kind of comment is actually a major opportunity.

Hence, the policy.

The first step in creating this policy is realizing that you're not always going to see constructive criticism when you first read it, because it's going to feel negative. Remind yourself of that in your policy by asking yourself, "Is this a negative comment, or is this person truly sharing their ideas in a constructive and helpful fashion?"

If it is the latter, then you should have a process of walking yourself through the proper response, even if your heart/mind wants to say something else.

In these cases, I like to reply with a comment in the avenue of, "Interesting idea. Thank you so much for the feedback. I'll keep that in mind for next time."

All they want to know is that they've been heard, especially when they went to the trouble of letting you know they think you could do better. Think about that. They think you can do better. That's a massive compliment! We should remember to take a compliment every now and again, even if we didn't get it the way we wanted it.

They could have just let us stay in our current state instead of trying to better us by leaving a positive/vanilla comment. In which case, we wouldn't have learned a thing.

Negative Comments

They happen. They're unavoidable. They are the sad side of the internet, and they are running rampant on YouTube. Negative comments will eat away at your soul. They're the things that we never wanted to hear. The complexes we never knew we had. The things that aren't at all true, but now we think they might be.

You can't let these stop you from doing your work. You can't even let them ruin your day. Respect the negativity in the world, because we all have a little bit. Some of us more than others. The people of the world, who live like victims, are going to take their sadness out on those who are doing something greater than just letting life happen to us.

You got this!

When I received my first negative comment, I was actually thrilled.

I know how crazy that sounds, so please humor me here. If I've learned anything about thought leadership, it's this: if you're not pissing someone off then you're not doing a good enough job of letting people know what you stand for.

That first negative comment was a welcome one because, at some point, you have to be a little concerned that everyone likes you. How is that niche?

Examples of negative comments could be, "This video sucks," or, "I don't know why my favorite YouTube channel recommended you. Not coming back," or, "Stop talking."

Ouch, right? It doesn't matter. You gotta have a policy in place for these instances. Simply ignoring it isn't going to get you far.

My policy, in this case, is to be apologetic, but not sorry. I believe if you created something for a reason and someone doesn't like it, you shouldn't be sorry you did it or mislead someone to think that you are. I will usually reply with, "Sounds like this video was not right for you. I invite you to come back and try the next one, or you're welcome to unsubscribe and not worry about it at all."

Hopefully, you read something specific in that response that I want you to think about. The reason everyone is afraid of their own comments section is that we believe everyone on the internet gets to share their true opinion, but we can't, so we're helpless. Every brand is going to be different and have a policy that reflects their internal culture, but let me tell you what mine is:

This YouTube channel exists because of my experience and opinion. If I'm allowed to give you tons and tons and tons of free value in the form of video content, I'm also allowed to have an opinion after the fact. I'm certainly going to defend my livelihood. For those people who are negative and not constructive with their approach, they get a big fat un-invitation from me. They have the right to share their opinion and I have the right to ask them to find something better if I'm not a good fit for them. Not my problem.

I don't think it's appropriate to stoop to their level, but I do think you have the right to stand up for yourself and should do it when necessary. Trolls should not feel like they have any reign over the internet. They should be put in their place. I'm not a believer in "if you don't have anything nice to say, don't say anything at all." I *am* a big believer in respect. Not everything that needs to be said is nice, but you can say it in a respectful way.

So, trolls, feel free to get a life and get off my lawn.

Inappropriate Comments

I'm sure it comes as no surprise that I get the occasional "show us your boobs" comments. I am a female. There are 12-year-old boys in their mom's basement being immature on the computer instead of doing homework. Online video is where this species migrates.

In these cases, you can create your own policy. In this example specifically, I will simply reply, "No." Letting them know that their comment has been seen and read can potentially satisfy them to keep going and do it again. Ironically, those people either never come back or suddenly become mature viewers and commenters. A normal person will see their mistake and go, "Oh my gosh, she read my comment," and correct their behavior.

I don't like to curse in my content (even though I seem to have no problem doing it in real-world conversations). There's something about putting four-letter words in writing that makes me a little sad inside, and it's the same when I say it on record in a video. When I see people reply with an F-bomb or something similar in the comments, I will kindly ask them to tone down the language.

Other occasions are unforgivable. Derogatory words toward a certain gender or ethnicity for any reason whatsoever get the boot entirely. I will block people from my channel for this reason. You have to do something pretty bad to get blocked by me, but this is a great example of pretty bad.

Nonexistent Comments

What worries me the most are the people who don't comment at all. I'm sure some people feel they won't be heard, simply want to observe the content, and then go about their day. I respect that. I just hope I'm doing right by them and they are happy with what they get from me. I'll never know until some serendipitous other occasion happens. Like meeting fans I've never seen in my comments at a conference in real life. Or someone reaching out to me who has been referred by someone who has been a long-time viewer. No comments. No emails. Just viewing.

I think it's sometimes important to just give a little nod to those people who aren't commenting to let them know you're listening to them, too. I try to encourage people to com-

> Immerse yourself in your community, because instead of waking up scared of your comments you'll truly understand the people who are there.

ment on a video by asking them to reply to a question. When I can, I'll mention to those who aren't commenting that I'm excited that they're skipping right to the part of taking action on what they learned from this video. Let everyone know that their thoughts and opinions matter, whether they are commenting or not.

As my friend Jay Baer says in his book *Hug Your Haters*, it's the non-commenters you need to worry about because, by staying quiet, they show that they are neither excited nor deeply upset by you. Even the ones who are upset can be won over because you have affected them so much that they left you a comment. If someone is middle-of-the-road and doesn't have a feeling one way or the other, you're just vanilla and forgettable. That's not why you're here.

The bottom line is that comments are important. We want them because they mean we are doing a great job of rallying a community. The comments are going to be good or bad. If there are too many bad, you need to look at what you might be doing wrong. If they are all good, you need to look at how middle-of-the-road your content might be. A thick skin is not your concern as much as understanding the trend of engagement. This is how you know whether or not you're accomplishing what you set out to do.

Immerse yourself in your community, because instead of waking up scared of your comments you'll truly understand the people who are there. You may not have a lot to work with in the beginning, but simply having the habit of watching for any and all comment activity will prepare you for the changing tides of opinion and personalities to come.

Show up. Continue the conversation. Don't just drop the mic. That's not how you build an effective brand.

Inviting Interaction

Comments are not the only way that we connect with our audience. There are many other ways, and it's critical to have interaction so that the video platform doesn't come off as a one-way conversation.

While at YouTube NextUp camp, they shared with us that interactivity is one of the big principles of a successful

YouTube channel. There are many more, of course, and you've heard them in some shape or form in this book, but this one resonated with me.

The shareability of a piece of content, as well as your presence as a whole, has so much more to do with a viewer's feeling of connection than it does about the content being good. Your video can be very, very good. Maybe even extremely helpful. However, if it doesn't drive an emotion of some kind, there may not be that urge to share with one's friends or community.

Don't get me wrong, a lot of people share my video content. The only reason I feel it could be even more successful is that interactivity is something I've struggled with over my career.

As a creator, I'm so proud and excited to share my knowledge and help as many people as I can. I think that has put me in the mindset that I have one job: to show up and deliver. Then, let people go on their merry way.

Sure I had CTAs and lots of encouragement to subscribe in some way. However, because I was encouraging viewers to take action on what they learned from our time together, I didn't want to pester them with some other form of interactivity. "Just get results." That's all I wanted for them *and* me.

After some deeper observation of the incredible creators doing it right and hearing why this would be an advantage for me, I realized that encouraging a next step with your viewers is not only appropriate but also a great way to make them feel even more a part of your community.

Community building is the name of the game. It's what makes people want to spread the word. They feel a sense of ownership that will have a crazy impact on your brand. Leverage that. Don't waste time letting your excited community do more to help you grow.

Let's go over a couple of ways you can continue to interact with your audience, in addition to or enhancing your comments section.

Enhanced Functionality

In the case of YouTube, the biggest platform of focus for this book, they obviously realize the importance of interactivity and therefore make it a priority to encourage it.

In the early days of the video sharing platform, two critical features helped engage audiences. One of them is gone, and the other is fading away.

The one no longer operating is the video response. Viewers could create a video in response to someone's content, upload it to their channel, and then submit it as an official video response to that original video. When approved by the creator, the response would appear underneath the first piece of content for viewers to watch.

Not only an opportunity for interactivity—this was face-to-face connection with video conversation before any of the other major social media platforms were even *thinking* about it—this was a great way for an otherwise undiscovered creator to start to gain some traction.

I should know. One of my favorite YouTubers to watch in the early days was Toby Turner. He always did this hilarious thing when he started an "iPhone channel" (a YouTube channel dedicated to uploading iPhone-recorded videos, so that the lesser quality wouldn't disturb the highly produced content on his main channel). He called this the Laziest Vlog Series, and would begin the video with his iPhone recording in an awkward position or place (like inside a trash can) and say, "Audience? Audience! What are you doing in the trash can?!" Then the vlog began.

I don't know what came over me one day. Maybe just being so thrilled by his hilarity and finally buying my first video camera. I decided to start a vlog the same way. I put the camera under my bed, lens facing out so you could see my feet walking up, and started with, "Toby? Toby! What are you doing underneath my bed?!" I went on to introduce myself, uploaded it to my YouTube channel, and then submitted that video as a response to Toby's latest lazy vlog. That was six years ago to the day that I'm writing this right now.

I remember waking up the next morning and grabbing my phone. I opened Twitter. There was an enormous amount (well, felt like a lot at the time) of tweets that were auto-generated by YouTube whenever someone liked my video. They read "I liked a @YouTube video from @ schmittastic Toby? Toby?! What are you doing? — Laziest Vlog Series video response."

There were so many of those tweets. I ended up with 4,000 views. I know there were a bunch of subscribers as well. For some reason, YouTube has lost that data. It was such a moment for me, because Toby had to approve that video for it to appear underneath his content for his own community to see. Then that community, as committed to loving and watching Toby as I was, watched me because of our common interest.

That was the first time I ever truly felt the effect of what interactivity could do. Not just for a creator, but for that creator's community.

I don't know how I lost touch with that over the years. Reminiscing about it now makes me so excited again. The average viewer in me kinda misses the simplicity and fun of a winning moment like that.

Now, unfortunately, the classic video response is no longer available. That doesn't mean you can't still do something similar to engage your audience. Also, at the time of writing this, YouTube is working on more robust social networking features for its creators. A richer audience interaction experience is always something that could pop up with the way social media relies on video these days.

Incorporating viewer video is still pretty simple to do, especially if you want to get creative in the content itself. Your audience *lives* to see their name—better yet, their face—in your video.

Whenever I want to incorporate viewer content, I ask them to upload a video in regard to the subject of my content to their own YouTube channel as "unlisted." This is essentially a way for outside viewers to watch a video through a link without it actually being public. (Private means that nobody except the logged-in creator can see a video, so unlisted is a middle ground.)

You can use third-party tools to download other YouTube channel content as a file to your computer. Then you can import it to your editor to integrate it into your final video project.

This is especially great for high-quality production Q&A videos. Having people ask a question on camera is a great experience for everyone involved. It's extremely interactive when you have an audience willing to engage enough to put themselves on camera for you.

This is even simpler with platforms like Snapchat, which is all the rage right now. Going to your community and asking them to send you their video questions in a Snapchat message is quick for them, though it's a little harder on your side because you need to have a screen recorder working in order to save that content (as Snapchat likes to make everything disappear). It's totally worth it to make it easy for the average user to ask a question, and you'll also be promoting your social channel in a way that's natural for the context of the video.

Okay. Went on a little bit of a tangent there because I love viewer video integration. Let's get back to that other enhanced functionality of YouTube that isn't quite dead yet, but leads us into a very important discussion: button pop-ups.

The first version of this that is still on YouTube today is called annotations. This function allows you to add what I like to think of as "buttons" to your video content. Like on top of it.

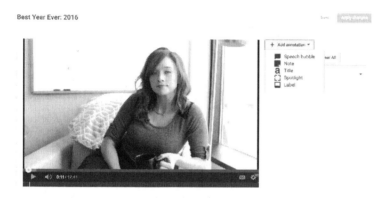

Being able to add a speech bubble or note with a text call to action gives an added reminder for your audience and even allows you to link to that action, depending on what it is.

The downside that has forever bothered YouTube creators about annotations is that they're kind of unprofessional-looking. Even worse, they're not mobile-friendly. When 50% of today's YouTube views are happening on mobile devices rather than desktop, you need more options.

They "fixed" the annotations issue by releasing YouTube Cards: the mobile-friendly, professional version of annotations.

Even if you're only uploading content at a basic level on YouTube, please, please, please immerse yourself in Cards. The level of interactivity and ratio of interaction offered is incredible. One of my favorite options of this feature is the ability to poll your audience.

This is enormously helpful. When your viewers feel a sense of ownership in what they're watching, they will absolutely chime in on your questions, especially when you make it this easy.

Cards are also measurable in YouTube analytics, which is amazing. You saw this poll example earlier, as well as the results, but I want to remind you because the bells should be going off about better engaging your audience. It's huge.

The other options for YouTube cards include what you see above in the drop down menu:

- Link to a YouTube video or playlist
- Link to a YouTube channel
- Encourage fans to fund your channel with donations via YouTube's tip jar feature
- Link to a non-profit donation opportunity
- Create a poll
- Link to an approved website

CAN I PULL THIS OFF?

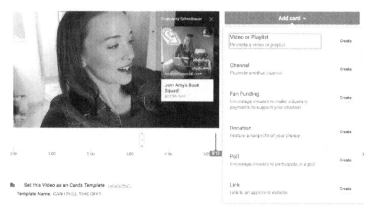

That last one is important. You'll also notice in the screenshot that there is a Card sticking out on the video. This was a Card I linked to a web page on my website for people to join my Book Squad. This was a place to sign up for updates about this very book as I was writing and publishing it.

The ability to link to your website is a big advantage with these interactivity features. You can only link to one site, and it needs to be the official website associated with your YouTube channel. Once it's linked, you can send people to any page on that website URL. Very simple.

YouTube continues to roll out more and more features to make it easy for you to engage your audience, including the latest development: end screens. This is an enhancement that helps you point viewers to subscribe to your channel and watch previous content. I literally can't even keep up with all the changes for this book. Things move so fast, but that's good news for you.

It can be difficult to get your audience to take action and engage. When you make the option super relevant and easy for them (not to mention simple for you to measure the return of that feature), it's a win-win for everyone. Your audience's connection to your brand will increase, shareability will pick up, and you will be well on your way to vlogging like a boss!

CHAPTER TEN
SUPERIOR SOCIAL MEDIA

Social media has done us a lot of favors over the years. We can become our own one-person business without changing out of pajamas. The ability to share what you're doing and find other people who will care is incredible.

But because of that, it also has its negatives. Social media isn't just a soapbox for you to give people links to click. People are there to have relationships with people. If they're following you, they're hoping for the same. The non-stop CTA of "watch my video" isn't going to be good. You should tweet that when you have a new video (more on that later). If it's the only thing you do on social media, then no one will care.

No one.

You have to remember why people are there and how you're going to fit into it all. Building trust is more than just amplification of content. It's engaging. If you want engagement (see the previous section), you gotta give it. That's how sharing your videos on social media is most effective.

We're going to talk about all the different ways you can share your content across different social, digital, and human platforms to grow viewers and brand awareness. But remember that this is only a small percentage of what you'll do on these platforms.

You're lucky to be invited to have the opportunity to share and ask for a click to your video. Building connections with people has to be your first priority. Always.

Facebook

It's a very interesting time for video because of platforms, like Facebook, putting so much skin in the game. If you're not up to speed on this (which must mean that you don't use Facebook at all), let me give you the scoop.

These days on the News Feed (the main feature of Facebook where people stay up-to-date on all things family, friends, ex-girlfriends, and brands), it is pretty much all video updates. Facebook is making it clear that they want you to upload video (and pretty much any media content) natively to their platform by pushing anything of that nature to the top of the News Feed. (If you're not familiar with the idea of "pushing it to the top," Facebook's News Feed is heavily impacted by an algorithm dictated by your own logged-in behavior. Your relationship with posts on your News Feed will determine what you see first. This makes it a very competitive game for those trying to get more eyeballs on their stuff.)

You can see where this might get sticky for someone who wants to be a YouTube creator sharing their links on Facebook. Not only is it going to be the opposite of what Facebook wants to see more of (native video content, not video linked off-site), but you're also using their biggest video marketing competitor.

How, then, does one effectively promote video content on Facebook? Let's go over your options.

Share the YouTube Link

If you're dead set on encouraging your Facebook community to either watch your YouTube video on Facebook or move over to the YouTube platform, you need to make that link share a little more enticing for Facebook to throw you a bone.

Amy Schmittauer
Published by Amy M Schmittauer [?] · August 14, 2016 · 🌐

Super fun visit to Facebook NY! Check out part 1 of my NYC trip:

VISITING FACEBOOK HQ | nyc part 1

SUBSCRIBE for part 2 and my YouTube NextUp NYC Experience! My Instagram Stories: http://instagram.com/schmittastic Vincenzo: http://yo...

YOUTUBE.COM

1,150 people reached   Boost Post

👍 Like   💬 Comment   ➦ Share

👍❤ Senouci Mohammed, Desiree Lopez and 21 others   Top Comments ˅

As you can see in this screenshot, Facebook doesn't do YouTube any favors when you post a link. My thumbnail is supposed to be a rectangle, and they've cropped it into a square—the tiniest, crappiest version of a link preview possible. This is what it looks like when you only post the YouTube link.

You can enhance your share by adding a native upload:

Amy Schmittauer
Published by Amy M Schmittauer [?] · January 1 at 12:10pm · 🌐

hello 2017!

https://www.youtube.com/watch?v=5dLC7hZdtqE

7,848 people reached   **Boost Post**

👍 Like   💬 Comment   ↗ Share   📷 ▾

👍❤ Prashant Patel, Aslan Yakut and 89 others   Top Comments ˇ

As you can see, this looks a little different. I've uploaded a photo as the main feature of the Facebook status update simply adding a few words and the YouTube link in the caption. It works the same way, but because the photo is a better experience for the users and technically a native media upload to the platform, Facebook lifts it up a bit more as my community engages with it.

You can see the difference here. This is an interesting example, because it has double the likes compared to the previous example (usually it's triple or quadruple). It has a tremendous amount of shares in comparison, in addition to engagement in the comments. This continues to drive the result higher in the News Feed as Facebook notes its popularity.

That ugly YouTube link just doesn't get the same traction or invite as much engagement, thus the lack of effectiveness in the share.

Upload Video Natively to Facebook

The previously mentioned practice of using the photo to enhance the YouTube link is my standard procedure. Every now and again I will upload a video directly to Facebook, another native upload option.

If you're not that partial to YouTube views and are more focused on creating videos to be seen no matter where the views are counted, in the beginning, your chances are much better on Facebook. Relatively.

There's something very important I hope you keep in mind for Facebook, YouTube, and any other social network you leverage. They are all extremely different.

For instance, your video on Facebook will appear on people's News Feeds. Super cool, right? That's what I call a "disruptive view." The viewer was stalking their friends and liking status updates when your video suddenly appeared and began to play. They did not make the decision to watch it by clicking a play button the same way they do for a YouTube video, an action I call an "intentional view."

The Facebook post route is going to elevate your views tremendously depending on how much reach you have. A person only needs to let your video play (with or without audio) on their News Feed for three seconds in order for it to count as a view for you (the metric as of this moment in 2017). It may seem like you're getting more views on Facebook, but that doesn't mean the quality of view is fantastic.

This is why I stress the importance of every social network being different. You might be wondering, "What's the big deal if I upload a video to YouTube and then try to get a little more reach by uploading to Facebook as well?" It's a great question, and you might think the answer is a no-brainer. If the feature is there, use it! Right?

Like I said, the factors that make someone think about clicking play on a YouTube video are wildly different from someone passively using Facebook. YouTube requires an incredible title because it's what you see to judge a video before you watch. On Facebook, you don't even see those things—although they are there—before the video is autoplaying in front of you, enticing you to watch thanks to the video content itself (without audio).

To simplify, I'll use myself as an example. You've probably watched me on YouTube at some point if you're this far into my book (and if not, that's super interesting). The majority of my content is considered *talking head* format (which basically means that I'm on camera in the same place throughout the video talking to you). A few overlays here and there, but mostly I'm a talking head.

Now, if you're watching on YouTube, you know we're having a lot of fun. But that is mostly because you can hear what I'm saying. If I upload a video in this format to Facebook where audio is only being turned on by the viewer about 15% of the time (yes, that's *it*), you wouldn't be so sure that the video is an enticing one to watch.

My content uploaded to YouTube performs significantly better than it does on Facebook. A video created for a specific platform is not guaranteed success across all platforms.

The answer to your question about uploading to both platforms varies. Did you customize the experience for both environments? Are you thinking like the viewer you want to attract in the context of their social experience? Will you do your video more justice by posting on one of these social networks over the other?

If a view is just a view to you, then Facebook is a great route. Not to mention, this is a sweet way to butter up the heavy-hitter social network to offer you a little more traction in the future. When you have a post that performs well (and video does, pretty much automatically), your page as a whole will get more attention from those who are engaged.

Brand awareness-wise, this is a win.

If YouTube and Facebook are of equal importance to you as tools to grow an audience, then feel free to have fun uploading your content in both places. As you can see, they are very much not the same thing.

Best of Both Worlds: Native Video and YouTube Link

Because the attention span on Facebook is ~~non-existent~~ extremely low, I like to take advantage of the fast-paced video while also encouraging people to click over to YouTube. Again, this is because I would prefer my views and community to grow in one place.

When I'm done with the video and it's live on YouTube, I will go back into my video editor and export a 15-second teaser. It can be the first 15 seconds of the video or the best 15 seconds of the video. Creating something that is not heavily reliant on audio (as the sound may not be turned on when they see it on Facebook), but is visually pleasing and fast-paced, is a great option for native upload to Facebook. Think of it as a video trailer customized for Facebook's environment.

I upload that 15-second clip to a status update with the link to the full version in the caption. I now have an effective promotion for my video that could make both platforms—Facebook and YouTube—happy.

The bottom line for Facebook is to remember context. Everything people are finding is in the News Feed, and they are a-scrollin'. What will you do to stop the scroll? That's the goal. (Hey, that rhymes!) When you've disrupted someone with your video, how will you visually pull them in and take them to another mindset?

Do that, and your Facebook promotional strategy for video will be on point.

A Facebook Exclusive Video Show

What if you read this book hoping to create a vlog with Facebook as your host platform? That's a 100% reasonable determination at this stage of social media and video. As you've read, Facebook is making video a huge priority, so why not leverage that opportunity?

I'm obviously a little biased toward YouTube, as that's where I've gotten my experience, but that doesn't mean it's the best tool for everyone.

I believe that if you have an existing network on Facebook, then it's an incredible place to start vlogging like a boss. The vlog is not just for YouTube.

My advice is to keep in mind what Facebook success looks like. You may not have the same strategies and goals as someone trying to achieve success on YouTube (see the information above on Facebook native upload vs. YouTube Links).

A visually compelling video project on Facebook is a massive responsibility for a video creator. Your viewers' eyes must keep moving, and you need to compel them to click your video and listen to get the full experience.

Watch those pages that are winning big with Facebook video and see how their content is bringing the heat with visual movement. What did they do to catch your eye? Probably not the same thing you would see on YouTube.

Does this mean that you can't have talking head videos? Absolutely not. The talking head format does not have to be a failure on Facebook, and neither do videos that are heavily dependent on audio.

The solution is captioning. Captions add a visual component to show the viewer what they are missing by not listening.

If you want to stand out on Facebook instead of contributing to the noise, don't automatically assume that your video will be a top performer if you upload it natively. It will do pretty well because of Facebook's generosity with views, but if you want to be a boss vlogger, you need to go the extra mile and make that content perfect for your viewer.

Twitter

Oh, Twitter. How I love thee.

I've been using social media platforms for some time. AOL tugs at my heartstrings a bit, because that was where I began my journey with social media. Myspace was an interesting stint of online learning. Facebook came into play. But then there was Twitter.

Whatever it is about Twitter that makes it so enjoyable (and the reason this may be starting to sound like a romance novel) must also be the reason the platform—although struggling financially—continues to win over its users.

Chronological social media updates are hard to come by these days when so many platforms are following the algorithmic model. I think that is why Twitter has so much staying power, and that's what makes it fantastic for video promotion. Even users who aren't promoting something would agree.

Twitter truly is a news feed. What Twitter calls the Home Stream is a timeline of all the tweets shared by the people you follow. It is *so* real-time that you might find out about an earthquake before you feel it because those who were hit first are already tweeting. That groundbreaking feature is still a special part of Twitter even ten years after its birth.

The upside for you video creators out there is that you can get your promo on without a ton of concern about coming off as spammy.

Now, do you want to remember you're talking to human beings here and try to be one yourself? Of course. But Twitter is incredibly fast-moving. Today's user has an average of 208 followers. So if you think about those followers who are following on average 150-200 accounts, a lot is going on.

Posting at different times of day in different contexts is important because you will probably get a tweet to someone who didn't see it the night before or a couple of days later. This is why I love Twitter. I don't have to be shy about sharing my links because I know the timeline is going to move fast enough that it's not a spam issue for my followers.

Best practice for Twitter is to share your video multiple times over a long period. You want your content to get as much exposure as possible and not just the first day the video goes live. You're investing in your archives for a reason, and that is why Twitter has become such a successful teammate of the YouTube creator. You can share something old on Twitter, and it might still be new to someone, so the date doesn't matter.

There are some third-party applications that are fantastic for sharing your content on Twitter. Some, e.g.

Hootsuite and Buffer, will schedule tweets. I also recommend Meet Edgar for a fantastic tool that will continue to tweet previously created tweets over a longer span of time, thus sharing your older videos and getting them new exposure without you having to do a lot of legwork.

The key thing is, again, to be human. Your Twitter account can't just be promotional tweets. New users, who are looking around and making a decision to follow you or not, are going to see that and quickly leave. The key to Twitter is engagement. The real-time opportunity to connect with people is the core of the platform.

So that means replying to people, whether they were starting a conversation with you or not. Dive into others' conversations and share your ideas. Twitter is 100% searchable (except for private accounts, of course). You can search a keyword within a geographical location and go to town on meeting new people (an awesome strategy for local businesses, by the way).

Twitter is also the modern day press release. Share what you're up to in 140 characters or less (this might change to unlimited characters, but I still say you should stay brief). Share a photo with a favorite moment of filming a video. Remember that people follow you in multiple places to get a different experience. Respect that policy and you will be worth a follow everywhere, just because. Not because you promoted the crap out of "all your social medias," as they say. (They being people who don't listen to their audience very well.)

In regard to sharing a video on Twitter, I treat it very similarly to Facebook: image and YouTube link. I can upload the video natively here, too. There is very little reason for that at the moment because I'm not trying to work an algorithm like I have to on Facebook. Twitter is starting to incentivize video creators, but still. I like my views on YouTube. Keep the CTA clean.

Here is a sample of what a Twitter promotion would look like with a photo and link:

Amy #VlogBoss @Schmittastic · 20 Nov 2016

so… people are quitting their vlogs… LET'S COLOR INSTEAD!

youtube.com/watch?v=n5Q76c…

Vincenzo Landino, Colorit, Aftermarq and Roberto Blake

↩ 5   ⟲ 14   ♥ 25   ⅼⅼ   • • •

What I love about photos on Twitter is that they add the ability to tag friends, similar to Facebook. Now, as you can see from this photo, no one else was in it or in the corresponding video. I tagged friends anyway. This is another great example of collaboration in the social media sector.

Remember: don't spam people. If you have a team of collaborators who love to share your stuff, tag them in the photo. They can see that it's live and they should retweet or share, watch, and comment. As you can see, it helps with your social proof. More importantly, it's encouraging teamwork and collaboration (which you need to offer to others just as much as you need to request it).

Otherwise, this is a very simple post. Caption, link, and photo. Boom. Shared.

When you see that post on your timeline, it should make you want to click. That's how you win over your real-time friends on Twitter.

Instagram and Snapchat

Facebook might be YouTube's biggest competitor right now, but another rivalry going strong in social is Instagram vs. Snapchat. Because these children are at odds, I put them together.

They do something similar in the way of offering users a more behind-the-scenes, exclusive look at what a creator is up to. At least, that's what the cadence of the platforms has been so far.

Let's start with the veteran: Instagram. It has a one-photo-at-a-time policy and no links except a single opportunity in your bio. It's always been a very clean experience. Facebook acquiring it made a lot of sense, because it highlights special moments in a user's life.

The simplicity of the platform encourages a little higher quality, which is why so many lifestyle and beauty influencers have grown huge businesses on the back of that content.

Then Snapchat was born. Slowly but surely, after rejecting Facebook's offer for their acquisition, they started to steal Instagram users. Offering a raw look into a publisher's mobile camera lens, Snapchat has an authentic behind-the-scenes feel. There was no ability to upload (at least in the beginning). You had to create your content in the app to share it.

Oh. Not only that, but everything about this app was private. There's not a lot in the way of discovery. Users have to know your username or scan a Snapcode to follow your Story, and private messages disappear immediately after being received. Discretion was a huge selling point until they started beating Instagram with in-app time. Privacy seemed to fall in importance, even though it's still technically a feature.

The two competitors have come head-to-head since Facebook decided to rip off the Story feature for their own Instagram app. Pretty much the same, except better.

Instagram makes you discoverable, both in your regular feed and your Story feed. Instagram made the video and photos cleaner, offered more flattering filters, and it made the raw version of you up to par with the visually pleasing nature of Instagram.

I had been on Snapchat for three years when this happened. The only reason I used it was because of the Story feature. I don't always want a photo to live on forever, but I still want to keep in touch with my community. When Instagram snagged the technology and I could leverage my existing following on the platform to build a similar rapport with them, I was 100% on board.

There is as yet no sign of Snapchat suffering from the competition, but the whole thing is still fascinating, particularly from a video creator perspective. You can get the benefit of similar features while choosing one or the other for your promotional presence, depending on your audience and where they like to hang out. Maybe you do need to be on both. Regardless, the strategies will be similar.

These platforms are your viewers' backstage pass. They want to know what you're up to outside of your usual video world, what it's like to be on set, how you spend your free time, and where you like to travel.

There is another important component of Instagram strategy: that one link in your bio. Remember—it doesn't have to be the same all the time. If you upload a photo teasing a new video, change the link and let people know in the bio. It's easy for people to click from there. Instagram is also trying to continue one-upping Snapchat by integrating link opportunities in the Story feature. Keep that in mind.

With Snapchat, you're going to have a little more difficulty getting conversion right away. I recommend you come up with a short link for whatever you're promoting and type it in the caption of your Snapchat Story. Encouraging people to screen capture your Snap will help them remember how to type the URL.

I think Snapchat might have to change this at some point to make it easier for creators and to keep up with the competition. For now, it may not be such a bad thing to nurture a following there and encourage viewers to take a more complicated step to watch your content.

Instagram and Snapchat are where you let people in. Be you. Share your version of behind-the-scenes. The core of the connection built between you and your community will happen in mediums like this.

No matter which platform you choose, or if you want to share on both, leverage these simple social networks to have that time with your audience outside of the structured, edited content you post. That alone will bring you incredible reach when a new video goes live.

Instagram or Snapchat Exclusive?

Could Instagram or Snapchat be your one-and-only choice for sharing video? Yes!

Snapchat was a big win when it arrived on the social media scene, because it took the basic idea of jump cut editing (which many vloggers on YouTube have become famous for, myself included) and gave it to the average smartphone video user to create their own version of a vlog via Stories.

Think about it. When you can only record one consecutive clip for ten seconds and are forced to stop and start again, that's similar to the fast-moving editing of YouTube vlogs.

The Stories feature in Snapchat and Instagram might be the only vlog you need. Little-to-no editing. Raw look. Tons of opportunity to get started quickly. Should you go for it? Although you might find your creativity restricted in some ways, I say you should give it a shot.

Too often we make the barrier to entry overly difficult and complex. I would prefer you start vlogging through Snapchat as your foray into the world of video than to never start at all.

Email Marketing

Don't you go skippin' this section. I mean it. You. I see you. Thinkin' about it.

Email marketing is not dead. This is a thing. Any YouTube veteran I have come into contact with who has asked me advice (which sounds funny when I have thousands of YouTube subscribers and they usually have millions), it is about email.

So many people build a platform on rented land. That's what social media is. That's what YouTube is. It's not yours. It can go away at any time.

Remember Myspace?

Think about that. Let's say you have 100,000 YouTube subscribers. You're uploading. Having a grand ol' time. People are viewing, commenting, and enjoying the connection they have with you every time you enter their subscription box.

Then *POW*. Google makes the drastic decision to shut down YouTube. And it's gone.

In an instant—no more YouTube subscribers.

This can happen anywhere. I'm just using YouTube as an example. I'm sure, like me, you're questioning the likelihood of such a crazy occurrence. The bottom line is that it doesn't have to go away altogether to have the same effect. Platforms change. Algorithms happen. Some brands were getting an incredible reach on Facebook a number of years ago, because the platform was (brilliantly) whetting the palates of prospective advertisers. Now it's nearly impossible to get an effective return without a little ad spend.

You do not control what you do not own.

That is why email marketing is so critical.

I have been using email, more specifically the AWeber email marketing service, since the beginning of Savvy Sexy Social in 2011. I've been an affiliate partner with the brand in recent years as we continue to find ways to work together. I'm always telling people about the importance of email marketing, and AWeber is always telling their users about the importance of video content. A perfect fit.

Because of their technology I have been able to grow a large email list of viewers, followers, friends, and anyone interested in learning more from me by getting content directly from the horse's mouth.

I have an invitation to the inboxes of thousands of people. YouTube only gives me that if they remember to email my video to my most engaged subscribers.

If I want to send an email when something is extremely critical—such as an important video release or, even better, a product for sale—I control that. My email platform is entirely mine. I acquire the contact information and set the tone of expectations.

People who have been investing in their YouTube subscribers for five to ten years are now seeing the value in growing an email platform to market their brand. It increases the sustainability of their own company and also grows their revenue stream opportunities, offering sponsors/advertisers/stakeholders an even greater opportunity for reach.

Other than mobile marketing—whether through acquiring phone numbers

> You do not control what you do not own.

or app downloads—email marketing is the best way to increase your owned assets. No matter what happens to a social platform you're relying on, your email list is a group of people who have made the ultimate offering of giving you their contact information. They will support you.

Do not waste time with this. Tools, like AWeber, are free to start. You can try out the interface of your liking. However, you must, must, must have an email list ready to grow from the start. This is too important to wait on. Just ask the YouTubers who went years without making a CTA and now can't find a way to integrate it into their approach or don't know how to grow effectively.

My advice is to leverage the copy in that description section and make a CTA. If you want people to join your list, let them know where they can do that. I also love using the YouTube Cards function for this because you can link to your website where they will find an opt-in form for your email list. That pop-up showing on-screen with you is the ultimate ask, especially when you verbalize it, but you already knew that.

Grow your owned assets and you'll sustain your brand. No matter what rocky social roads are to come.

PART THREE
KILL IT LIKE A BOSS

CHAPTER ELEVEN
CAMERA CONVERSATION

Note: As much as I want to help you with equipment advice, I also want to make sure you have updated information. Instead of reading about cameras that might be extinct by the time you read this, you can always find the most recent list of equipment I recommend at savvysexysocial.com/shop.

It seems weird for a book about video to wait so long to talk about equipment and production, huh? I know. I want to talk before we dive in.

At first, I wasn't going to have a gear chapter at all. With all my experience in video creation over the years, I've learned that equipment is never the real reason people don't get started or continue with vlogging. I didn't want to glorify a misconception by going into detail about equipment that will probably retire this book faster than I can get it published.

Then I started thinking about what it was like for me to get started with video.

I remember those super early days after the wedding video. I wanted to dive in, but I thought, "If only I had a good enough camera...." Hard to judge you for something I know I did.

The kicker was how I did my research to find the best camera. I watched hours and hours of vlogs from my favorite creators (you'll hear about them in the next chapter), waiting for them to say the name, make, or model of their camera. I wanted what they were using. I waited for the moment they would stand in front of a mirror so I could pause the video and watch frame-by-frame for what they were using.

Back in '09, there weren't so many resources talking about what tools to use for YouTube video. It was barely seen as a legitimate outlet, much less one people were teaching about.

The crazy thing was that I already had what most of the top vloggers were using: that Canon Powershot. Maybe I had an older model, but that was it. That was the choice camera for video on YouTube.

It took me forever to figure that out. I didn't even know for sure until after I had already started creating and even bought my first handheld video camera. (This was before smartphones killed them all). The Flip. The Kodak Zi6. This is what I started with because I would discover them online and give them a shot. Nothing ever did video right the way the Canon Powershot did.

After reminiscing about that in my head and thinking about how hard it was for me, I started to reconsider a gear chapter. It may be easier for you today, but that doesn't mean that you don't want a recommendation from the person who just laid out an entire content plan for your video channel.

That's why there's a chapter at all, but I saved it for near the close because of the brainstorming and planning we've already done. You might have a big plan for your YouTube channel now. Maybe you're more inspired to have a show on Facebook. Whether it's one of those two, Snapchat, Instagram or any of the social networks that will pop up for years to come, you have to use the tool that makes the most sense for each place.

I hope that you're so well-versed on who your perfect viewer is and what they want to know that you have a clear vision of what your vlog looks like for them. What camera is going to do you justice? Does the audio setup need to be special for some reason? What about your set? Where will you film: in one place or many? There are so many things to consider, and your equipment decisions must work within the context of that plan. Therefore I can't make the decision for you.

I will give you my best recommendation at this moment in time, when accessibility to video is the best and highest quality it's ever been.

Let's start with the camera that I'm 98% sure you already have.

Smartphone Video

Whether you're an iPhone or an Android or a Windows, you've got that microcomputer in your pocket.

We talked about how incredibly powerful this little guy is in the section about the fear of gear. Hopefully, by now you're on board, especially after you've heard all the details of social video and how your plan fits into that world. Quick and easy video is relatable for your audience, so why wouldn't it be a great option?

Look, you know what to do. Open the camera app and start capturing video. It's that simple. If you want to step up quality (so you're not just relying on perfect conditions and a steady hand for the near future of your video career), I have a couple of tips to help you put your best foot forward with what you have.

Upgrade your footage with camera accessories.

Such amazing tools are created for smartphones to improve your video quality (for not too much money). There are ways to upgrade the lens to different types of view, like a wider angle or fish-eye. You should think about an additional external microphone, so that you're not relying on what's built-in. Get a tripod. Just because you're on a smartphone doesn't mean you can't have a steady setup—especially when you're run-and-gun filming on your own.

Get cloud storage ready.

You don't want all these video files sitting on your phone, especially if it's the phone you use reg-ularly. Create a Dropbox, Box, or Google Drive account, and download their apps to your phone so that you can quickly and easily upload your video footage. You can also opt to upload the video files to YouTube directly in private and download the mp4 from the backend for further editing. Free storage!

Always, always, always look at the lens of the camera.

Ideally, you're using the rear-facing camera of your smartphone (opposite side of your screen), which is the highest quality. The front-facing camera (same side as your screen) is a good option as well and continues to get better with each new phone release. But for less-seasoned video personalities, it's easy to look at yourself and not the lens of the camera while filming. Later we're going to talk about how vital it is for you to look in the right place when you're filming. I want to make sure you keep that in mind for smartphone video, because it's an easy thing to screw up and a major disconnect for the audience.

How exciting is it that you now have permission to just whip out that phone whenever something cool is happening (even when that something cool is you sharing an idea on your vlog)? You should be very excited, because your audience is already.

Cameras

As I said before, the Canon Powershot has been one of the go-to cameras for many vloggers on YouTube for a long time—even when smartphone video became as good or even better than the Canon.

The reality is that when you're an avid video creator, getting a text while you're trying to vlog is a pain. Storage, both in restriction of space and ease of importing, is an issue to think about as well. Not to mention the times when you're vlogging about something that you need to see or share on your phone. That happens all the time. These are just a few reasons that smartphones will continue to be less effective than cameras.

So the handheld vlogging camera continues to be a selling item for those hardcore creators.

No matter who the manufacturer is, vloggers are looking for something compact and easy to operate. Just because you're a pro doesn't mean you need to have crazy complicated equipment. For on-the-go video, I'm using an updated version of what the Powershot always did for me.

For a long time, I was using the same camera in the studio as I did on-the-go, because that's what you do when you're first starting. Whatever you have, you use.

After a few years, I upgraded to a DSLR camera (again, Canon) for in-studio filming. There was a bit of learner's curve regarding how to properly operate a professional grade camera. It also made some things easier, such as making sure my head was in the frame and getting the audio quality I wanted.

Audio

What? Audio? What's that got to do with video? *Everything.*

It's incredible how much we can get away with crappy video these days, even with the advancements in smartphones. If your audio isn't quality, your video is as good as dead.

In most cases, you'll be fine. The built-in microphones on cameras aren't terrible. If you're starting to take this seriously, you don't want to end up in the situation of getting that awesome video captured and relying on audio that's going to be a little iffy.

Say, for instance, that you're filming outside. What if it's windy? That smartphone microphone is going to sound like crap. Maybe your fancy camera setup is amazing and looks great, but it also means the tripod is ten feet away from you in a room with hardwood floors and nothing on the walls. No bueno. That's echo-city.

When you vlog, you need to be aware not only of what can be seen in the frame, but what can be heard. Do you know how many times I accidentally put my finger on top of the microphone on that Canon Powershot? Too many.

Does the camera you're using allow for external audio attachments? Maybe that would be a good base to cover. If not, what will be the designated purpose of this camera and what circumstances are going to require you to step up to something that's a little more professional?

Choosing audio equipment is a daunting task but you have to do it. For any moment you remember watching someone's video and the harsh wind or unbalanced volume displeased your ears, don't let that be you.

Lighting

Here's the good news. This is something you can put off spending your money on for a while. I did. I didn't buy a light for my setup until years after getting started.

What did I do in those early days? Well, grasshopper, there's this thing called the sun....

No, really. Natural lighting can totally work. (*My video nerd friends are cringing right now, but that's okay. Let them.*) Not everyone is interested in a fancy filming situation. Quite frankly, it might not be the most relatable thing to your audience anyway.

The first hundred or so episodes of Savvy Sexy Social were dependent on sitting next to a window in my office between the hours of 2:00 and 4:00 pm. That was when the sun was just right, and I had enough lighting to knock out my video pretty easily.

Was the lighting consistent throughout? Not always. Was it perfect? Definitely not. But I didn't care. The video had to be made, and a three-point lighting setup was not in the budget.

Eventually, I bought a small, cheap, LED panel to balance the light on the other side of my face. Also started to help with aging. (*Ladies, do you hear me?*)

Today, I still rely mostly on natural lighting at a certain time of day, but I also use a light for my face and something to brighten up my background. But when I'm vlogging on-the-go, that's going to be lit based on the context of the situation. That's okay.

Figure out your vlogging story, and the lighting situation will become clear to you. If you choose a place to film regularly that needs a little help in the brightness department. Then start shopping for your options. If you can get started with what the sun gives you on a daily basis, then I approve. That's how I roll.

Editing

As a beginner in the editing world today, you have so many options. You don't even have to leave your smartphone to edit a video anymore.

If you're seriously considering a smartphone-only vlogging life, then go to town on editing tools in your relevant app store. There are hundreds, maybe even thousands, to choose from.

If you want to edit on the computer, because that might drive you slightly less crazy, I have a few recommendations.

First and foremost, you should start with the editing program that may have come with your main computer. It will get the job done in most cases. As you know, I started editing with Windows Movie Maker. Yes, I tried to get away from that as quickly as possible. *Hey. It might be a good tool today, but I grew out of it quickly.*

If you don't have software and don't want to buy any yet, there are websites that allow you to edit. (YouTube is the one I would recommend trying first.) Uploading your footage in private mode and then using their drag and drop editor would be a great way to get started. It's not going to give you a ton of room to be creative, but there are plenty of tools to enhance your video.

If you want to purchase editing software, you can always look into some intermediate options out there. There are many you can get your hands on for around $100. They will probably decrease in price as this industry continues to shift.

But if you're going to get serious with video and you're ready to buy editing software, you might as well go big and get the pro level. You don't need to know how to use every little thing. It's better to grow into a platform rather than have the learner's curve of a new one every time you need to upgrade.

There are so many options to consider for video, from camera gear to software and a lot more. You'll feel the pressure to continue to improve your video arsenal. Just remember that you should recognize your need for these things as it occurs. I nerd out on different audio options, lights, editing plugins, branding, and a ton of things in between, but I don't buy something unless I know I'm going to use it.

Otherwise, you end up with a lot of gear and little execution. Prove you need it.

Production

I have not spent a lot of time talking about video production in this book. That is for one simple reason: it's not necessary.

The beauty of vlogging is that there aren't strict rules for how to do it "right." You can position a camera however you like and frame yourself on screen the way it feels best. If you do everything it takes to give your perfect viewer the value they deserve, then that's the most important thing.

However (because I know you're going to ask), I will offer you a few pieces of advice about production quality.

1. Pay attention to how much of your body is in the frame.

    If you're too far away from the camera and your entire body is in the frame, that's going to feel unnatural to viewers. It's nice to have full body shots to change the perspective now and then. For the most part, we're talking to a person as if they're sitting down for coffee with us. We don't see an entire person's body when we're having a conversation. Our viewpoint usually falls between the top of the head and the upper body. If you want your video to feel like it's an intimate conversation, frame about that much of your body for the majority of the video. There's also such a thing as *too* close, such an up-the-nose shot. Be aware of your most flattering view.

2. Avoid too much space above your head.

    Just like it's unnatural to talk to someone face-to-face while seeing their entire body, it feels weird to see a lot of space above their head. It's incredibly distracting to watch a video when the person only appears in the lower half of the camera frame and the rest is dead space, just walls and ceiling.

    I may follow this advice a little too strictly, as I'm more likely to cut off my own head (just a little bit) than have space above it. Find your happy medium—which will depend on where you're filming—and keep the space around you in mind.

3. Set the lens of your camera at eye level or slightly above and tilted down.

    Speaking of up-the-nose, let's dig into camera flattery a little bit more. Again, we want this to be like a natural conversation. The rule of thumb is to set your camera up so that the lens is at your eye level, always taking production points one and two into consideration. Eye level is a good place to be.

    That being said, some of us like to take into consideration how much weight the camera "adds." The best way to avoid video-weight-gain is to have the lens of the camera slightly higher than your eye level and tilt the camera down. This slims your face and pretty much everything else. You'll feel much better reviewing yourself on camera if you're not judging your appearance too harshly at the same time. This little camera trick works beautifully. (Witness all the selfies of people holding their smartphone cameras high in the air and looking up at the lens.) It's a sneaky, but effective, way to avoid a double chin. We all have one. It just depends on where the camera sits.

4. Record a few tests on your camera and look at them on a computer in full screen.

    The bummer of filming is that when you import your footage into the computer, you almost always see dirty laundry in the background or discover that you cut your head off. Before filming the real deal, make sure you test the shot and view it on a big enough screen to know if you need to make any adjustments. Once you film in a spot on a regular basis, you will know what you need to do to get the framing just right and won't need as many tests. Remember, you can't always trust the tiny viewfinder to make sure everything looks okay. If you don't test first, you will probably regret it later.

5. Pay attention to the audio.

Poor audio will kill a good video, so keep that in mind while you're filming as well as when you're editing. One thing people forget to do with audio is to edit it so that the sound flows nicely. When you drag and drop clips together, you can often hear the start and stop of new audio between each clip when you're listening to the final edited version. If it's a jarring experience for the viewer, the rest of the video will not feel professional.

Be aware of that, and search for some adjustment tools in your video editor that will smooth out the audio and make it feel like one fluid experience (many audio editing tutorials are available online).

6. Be aware of camera output quality.

It pays to know your way around your camera if you're planning to edit on a more professional level. For instance, if your camera records at 30 frames per second in 1080p HD quality, then make sure that when you're exporting a final project from your video editor that the settings of your project are set the same for the final export.

The reason you need to do this is that your edited video is essentially a new video, therefore your editing software will do whatever you tell it to—potentially without taking the details of your actual footage into consideration. Things start to look a little less quality when you export a video that has different settings than the footage you used, downgrading the visual quality considerably. It's silly to spend all that time shopping for a camera based on its specifications only to lose out in post-production.

7. Make mistakes. Then, learn from them.

    Even after more than 1,000 videos published online, I find that there are always little things in production quality that could have been better. These problems weren't worth holding a video back from publishing. Allow yourself to learn from mistakes because they will keep happening. Unless it's a total loss (like, you forgot to turn on the microphone while you were filming...been there), then try to push through and see if it's salvageable. If you can do it again, give it a go.

CHAPTER TWELVE
THE SECRET

I don't know how exactly you ended up here, but here you are.

Maybe you've seen a video I created. Maybe you heard about me through a friend. Maybe we knew each other at one time. You made it all the way to this point because, on some level, you care about connecting with your community the same way I care about connecting with you.

That spark is incredible, right? Someone who is encouraging, helpful, and insightful helps you see the opportunity to make your mark in the world as well.

I know how you're feeling. As hesitant as you are about some things, you see so many amazing opportunities as well. That's how I saw it when I was inspired by the creators who paved the way for people like me.

In my early days of being a viewer, many inspired me, but just a few who I could call my favorites.

Philip Defranco is someone I watched very closely for a lot of years, and he was a major inspiration for Savvy Sexy Social. He knows how to take something that might ordinarily not be of much interest to young people (such as the news, politics, or other things that would be easier to tune out altogether) and makes it interesting. You're a little bit smarter when you leave.

What inspires me is his ability to jump cut information so that before you know it, you've learned something new, and you had a great time doing it. I wanted to share that same experience with the viewers of Savvy Sexy Social, and that was the basis of the content for those beginning years when I was a nobody in the marketing world and needed to talk quickly to get on people's radar to grow my brand. I stood out because I took a topic businesses wanted nothing to do with and found to be a chore (social media marketing) and made it fun and easy to learn about.

Another creator who holds a special place in my heart is Justine Ezarik, better known as iJustine. This young lady has also been on YouTube since its very early beginnings and continues to rock her channel. Justine taught me what it's like to take something completely mundane and otherwise uninteresting and make it a ridiculously fabulous time.

I also learned a lot from her on the technical side of creating videos, whether she was doing a tutorial on equipment or I was pausing at just the right moment to find out what camera she used. She was the person who encouraged me to buy my first handheld video camera.

Then there's Grace Helbig. Grace is also an incredibly fun time and talks about whatever happens to be interesting or trending, but her differentiator hit home for me. She showed me how okay it is to be the awkward-older-sister-type and that even we have a place where people can appreciate and feel connected to us. That was huge for me personally. No one likes to be awkward until you learn how to embrace it in your own weird and awesome way.

Last, but not least, Gary Vaynerchuk. I may not have seen him as a video mentor until later in my experience, but the way he is taking the vlogging world by storm to show a different side of the business is incredible. He also leveraged video to promote his family wine business before anyone thought YouTube was legitimate, landing him on talk shows such as Conan and Ellen.

You read how much he inspired me to think outside of the video box, vlog like a boss, and get attention. That only worked because I took inspiration and turned it into action. Now, one of my greatest business idols knows me by name and sees the mark I'm leaving on the world.

Inspirational people touch us every day. What matters is what we do to nurture those relationships and keep connections going. I was so fortunate that when I started, my digital mentors were uploading content on this thing called the internet so regularly that I felt I could live through them. They taught me so much and got me started. That's the spark.

You Can Do This

This is the part where I usually share an inspirational quote. I want you to seriously think about taking action and being empowered enough to make this happen. I always feel inclined to share some amazing insight that someone smarter than me said so that their advice can reflect how I feel for you right now.

Instead, I'm going to tell you what is top of mind for both of us at this moment, the moment you're considering making videos for the first time or maybe just a little more often.

You need to know that you can do this. You need to know that you can make it happen.

When you do, your first videos are going to suck.

That's right. That's my motivation bomb for you.

They're going to suck. It's okay. Laugh about it now. Be a little afraid. Brace yourself. Know that it's true. Get over it. Your videos are going to suck.

At first.

Because you've gone through this process to educate yourself on how to do the best you can with each and every upload, you're better off than many. Some creators have been uploading sucky content for as long as they've been crazy enough to do so. Crazy because they don't stop to look and see what the root of their problems are. They just keep doing what they think is right.

Before I wrote this chapter, I had a lengthy conversation with my dear friend and long-time YouTube creator Adande Thorne (better known as Swoozie to his community of 4.5 million subscribers, who are better described as his close friends if you see the kind of content he shares).

We've been known to have long conversations. When people are as busy as we are, but also have *so* much to say, talks become lengthy, intellectual, and somewhat deep. I started calling them private podcasts because the amount of knowledge we share with each other would be the most incredible teaching opportunity for new creators if it were published content. But, ya know, if we had time.

So, during this particular call, I shared my hypothesis about certain metrics (subscribers and views), explaining how I hate it when people decide that these numbers dictate a YouTube channel's real success. On some level, those numbers do matter. I asked him if he'd noticed what happens when a channel starts to see a lower ratio of views to subscribers.

He immediately cut me off and asked, "Do you want to know the secret?"

I stammered, "Yes, of course," because everyone likes to hear a secret,

"The secret to this whole thing is looking at what you created and asking yourself, 'Would I share this?'"

Would I share this? Seems silly, right? Like, of course I would share this! It's my video!

Think again. If you took a step back and looked at your project objectively, would you share your video for any other reason besides the fact that you created it? That you're in it?

Would you share it? Would you rave to your friends about it? Would you post it on all of your social media channels with the caption "OMG this is a must-see!" so that everyone can enjoy it with you? Is it *that* good?

"If the answer is yes, you're on your way. If the answer is realistically no, you're in trouble," he said.

See, Swoozie's point was that even when you've created great videos and some level of success, it's easy to get too comfortable and rest on your laurels.

So, even though your first video is not going to be that great, if you can objectively think about it or watch it back and think, "Yes, I would share this for other reasons outside of myself," you're better off than many. The trick is holding on to that mentality for every upload.

There have been plenty of times that I simply uploaded a video because I thought the idea was cool and I was on a deadline. You will have those days. You're not going to get it right every time, but each upload is a massive learning experience. Which is why you need to stay consistent and continue to create: you will always have something to learn.

The perspectives that matter are from your ideal viewers. They're your inspiration, case study, content approval source, and fuel for the next video. And the next one. And the next one.

You don't create a perfect viewer persona for the fun of it. It's the driving force behind everything you execute, or at least the things that matter. If a colleague says they don't like what you're doing, forget it. If your parents don't quite understand, that's okay. I'm sure you can think of someone or a group of people right now that may make you a little uneasy when you think about them watching you on video.

Are they part of your niche audience? If they are, then what would make them love it? If they aren't, they were only going to give you sympathy views anyway. Focus on your target audience and work very hard. It will pay off.

Your relevancy can shift in a single upload. All it takes is one. But that one may only come after many other uploads. First, you need to get through the ones that suck.

Remember your why? I hope it's feeling strong right now. Because the urge to create something that people will love should be jumping out of your skin, if this is the creative outlet for you. You're ready to let the world see you at your best. You're ready for a better platform that expresses the good you want to do in this world.

All you have to do to get started is click record. Then publish.

Lights. Camera. Action. You're ready to vlog like a boss!

ACKNOWLEDGMENTS

There are so many people who have made me who I am today, one moment at a time. I wish I could acknowledge everyone.

To my mom, Jacquie. It is so fun being a version of you. Thank you for letting me find my way even though it may not have been your plan for me. The life skills you taught me have been my greatest assets to date. My most precious goal is to make you proud of me, and I will continue to strive for that every day. I love you.

To my dad, John. Thank you for asking to be my dad. That makes me proud to carry your name all over the world. You are the most extraordinary example of a husband, father, and friend, and I couldn't be happier to be your daughter. Also, thank you for encouraging me to make my bed every day. Turns out that does matter. A lot. I love you.

To my fiancé, Vincenzo. No one has stood by me and believed in me as much as you. I never thought I would find someone who could be a life partner and a best friend.

You are both of those and everything in between. I can't wait to spend my life with you. I love you.

To my sisters and brothers, Kari, Johnny, Jimmy, and Jamie. How far we've come! You are each a reminder to me of how special, weird, and incredibly valuable family is. Thank you, and I love you.

To my ~~dog~~ best friend, Lucy. I wouldn't be the adult I am today if I hadn't adopted your cute puppy face at the age of 18. Thank you for growing up with me and being my unconditional best friend. Being your mom has been the hardest job and the greatest blessing I've had so far in my life. Thanks for pushing through with me. I wouldn't be here without you. I love you.

To my godmother, Aunt Maria. Thank you for always being supportive of me. One thing I treasure deeply is the relationship you and mom have. It's an incredible example of family friendship that inspires me every day to be a better sister. I love you.

To Sara. I don't know why we took so long to find each other as friends, but I am grateful beyond words. Thank you for "getting" me. You're the close girlfriend I never thought I could have. Love you.

To Jesse. Your positivity and belief in me continue to blow me away. I don't know why you thought I was special that day we met, but thank you for seeing that in me ever since. No one advocates for me harder than you, and for that, I'm eternally grateful. Also, no matter how much of a poker face I have, you are one of the funniest people I know. Keep doing your art. Love you.

To Jess. My "sister"! Thank you for being an incredible light in everything you do. Your hardworking, no-bull attitude is the reason I've always felt so close to you on this business journey. You help me in more ways than you will ever know. Love you.

To Matthew. You're the best thing that ever came out of a road trip across the country. I'm incredibly fortunate to call you my friend and confidant. Thank you for continuing to root for me and hold me accountable.

To Chris. Thank you for believing in me enough to watch an online video and invite me to speak in the Philippines. That was one of the most groundbreaking and important moments of my career. All because you took a chance on me. Thank you.

To Social Authority members. Thank you for being the savviest group of creators and businesses that I could have surrounded myself with on this journey. You amaze me.

To AWeber. Thank you for being the biggest advocate and friend of Savvy Sexy Social. Your willingness to work with me and help me grow is something I'm incredibly grateful for. Thank you for sponsoring this book and helping make my dream come true.

To the many who have helped me throughout my career in some big or small way, I wish I could name you all. Stephanie, Alison, Austin, Adande, Stevie, Christin, Terry, Nathan, Sue, and Michael, thank you.

To Columbus. I couldn't be prouder to be a resident and advocate of this beautiful city. Thank you for being my home.

To the "Socials." I am humbled by how much you lift me up. Thank you for listening to my words and thank you for taking action. I wouldn't be here today if not for you doing the work and showing the world what you're made of. Never give up, keep making videos, and **go after what you want.**

ABOUT THE AUTHOR

Amy Schmittauer is the Vlog Boss at Vlog Boss Studios and creator of the YouTube channel Savvy Sexy Social. YouTube selected her channel as a winner of their NextUp creator program, and *Business Insider* named her one of the 2016 up-and-coming YouTube stars you should be watching right now. An internationally acclaimed keynote speaker, Amy has also received high marks at the most influential digital events around the globe. She lives in her hometown of Columbus, Ohio. Connect with Amy at SavvySexySocial.com.

Step up. Stand out. Create Video.

It's time to share your message with the world!

Vlog Boss University will show you how to design your video success formula so that you can spread your message and grow a community of advocates for life.

Vlog like a *boss* and create the life you want!

Start Vlog Boss University at the level that best suits you. We have beginner, intermediate, and advanced online training programs available.

Ready to get started? Step up and make it happen!

Visit
www.VlogBossUniversity.com

Bring Amy To
your business or organization

YouTuber. Keynote Speaker. Author.

Amy Schmittauer is the Vlog Boss. A new media triple threat—YouTuber, keynote speaker, and author— she coaches people to go after the life they want and leverage online video to make it happen. Amy's genuine approach and actionable guidance offer a new kind of speaking experience for your audience.

An internationally acclaimed public speaker, organizers have praised her as a "professional" who "enthralls" the audience and is "easy to work with."

Contact Amy about your event:
SavvySexySocial.com

Made in the USA
Columbia, SC
04 May 2018